Prospects

An Advanced Course Student's Book

John Percil & Joanna Gray

Penguin Books

PENGUIN BOOKS

Published by the Penguin Group
27 Wrights Lane, London W8 5TZ, England
Viking Penguin Inc., 40 West 23rd Street, New York, New York 10010, USA
Penguin Books Australia Ltd, Ringwood, Victoria, Australia
Penguin Books Canada Ltd, 2801 John Street, Markham, Ontario, Canada L3R 1B4
Penguin Books (NZ) Ltd, 182–190 Wairau Road, Auckland 10, New Zealand
Penguin Books Ltd, Registered Offices: Harmondsworth, Middlesex, England

First published 1988

Copyright © John Percil and Joanna Gray, 1988
All rights reserved

Printed and bound in Great Britain by
Hazell Watson & Viney Limited
Member of BPCC plc
Aylesbury, Bucks, England

Except in the United States of America, this book is sold subject to the condition that it shall not, by way of trade or otherwise, be lent, re-sold, hired out, or otherwise circulated without the publisher's prior consent in any form of binding or cover other than that in which it is published and without a similar condition including this condition being imposed on the subsequent purchaser

ACKNOWLEDGEMENTS

The publishers make grateful acknowledgement to the following for permission to reprint copyright material:

'The Marriages Most Likely to Succeed', *Living Magazine*, September 1985, page 5; 'The Lesson We Refuse to Learn', Royce Logan Turner, *The Guardian*, 14 July 1986, page 24; material adapted from *Appointments in Administration 1986*, Civil Service Commission, 1986, page 30; 'Reaping a Whirlwind', © *Daily Telegraph*, 3 June 1985, page 38; 'Common Sense', *Collected Poems 1952–83*, Alan Brown, Martin Secker & Warburg Ltd, page 48; 'Things I Wish I'd Known at 15', Paul Young, © D. C. Thomson & Company Ltd, 1985, reproduced by permission from *Jackie*, issue dated 1.6.85, page 62; 'Touch', Hugh Lewin, in *Poets to the People: South African Freedom Poems*, Barry Feinberg (ed), Heineman Educational Books, 1980, page 64; *Teaching as a Career*, H. C. Dent, Batsford, 1961, page 73; *How to Survive Matrimony*, Herald Froy, Frederick Muller (an imprint of Century Hutchinson Ltd), 1950, page 79; *The Idea of Politics*, Maurice Duverger, Methuen & Co, 1966, page 89; *Whitehall: Tragedy and Farce*, Clive Ponting, Sphere, 1986, page 108; *Ways of Seeing*, John Berger, BBC and Penguin Books, 1972, page 124; *The Limits of Science*, Peter Redawar, Oxford University Press, 1986, page 138; 'Memorial Tablet', Siegfried Sassoon, by permission of George Sassoon, page 142; 'Computer Software for Working with Language', by Terry Winograd, *Scientific American*, September 1984, page 151; *All in the Mind*, John Nicholson and Martin Lucas (eds), Multimedia Publications (UK) Ltd, 1984, page 169; *How Children Fail*, John Holt, Penguin Books, 1984; 'The Origin of the Solar System', from *Biology and Hygiene*, E. J. Ewington and D. F. Moore, Routledge & Kegan Paul, 1971; 'The Pedestrian', Ray Bradbury, reprinted by permission of Don Congdon Associates Inc, copyright © 1951 by Ray Bradbury, renewed 1979 by Ray Bradbury; 'What I Believe', Bertrand Russell, in *What I Believe*, Mark Booth (ed), Waterstone Press, 1985; 'The Breadwinner', Leslie Halward, from *Forty Short Short Stories*, Edward Arnold, 1965; 'Life and Careers on the Football Terraces', Peter Marsh in *Football Hooliganism: the Wider Context*, Inter-Action Trust, 1976; 'The Secret Life of Walter Mitty', James Thurber, Hamish Hamilton, 1942, © James Thurber, © Helen and Rosemary A. Thurber, Harcourt Brace Jovanovich (US publishers); *Messing About with Problems*, C. Eden, S. Jones, and D. Sims, Pergamon Press, 1983.

The publishers make grateful acknowledgement to the following for their permission to reproduce copyright photographs and illustrations:

Melanie Friend, p. 9; Susan Griffiths, pp. 14 (Fortnum & Mason) and 100 (G. Baldwin & Co); National Maritime Museum, p. 15; Steve Richards, pp. 27 top, 44, 45 top and bottom, 46 and 47 bottom right; Tish Murtha, p. 27 bottom; cartoon, p. 28, reproduced by permission of *Punch*; Mel Calman, cartoon p. 32 right, and p. 158; D. W. Design, cartoon p. 32 left, artwork pp. 76 and 77, cartoons p. 78, artwork pp. 140 and 143; Rupert Besley cartoon p. 40; Daisy Hayes, p. 47 top and bottom left; Mike Wells/Aspect, p. 50 top; Orde Eliason/Link, p. 50 bottom; Mary Evans Picture Library, p. 59 left; Camera Press, pp. 59 centre, 80 top and centre, 81 top, and 112 bottom; The Mansell Collection, p. 59 right; Andrew Besley, p. 80 bottom; Popperfoto, pp. 81 bottom, 95 right and 155; Wolverhampton Art Gallery/The Bridgeman Art Library, p. 82; Rodmey Prynne, cartoon p. 93; Ingram Pinn, 'Blinded by Trivia', p. 98 (Leeds Postcards); Janet de Wagt, 'Women Against the Nuclear Threat', p. 99 top (Leeds Postcards); Jill Posener, p. 99 bottom; Barnaby's Picture Library, p. 111 top; Australia Information Service/Alex Ozelins, p. 111 bottom; Hans Holbein, 'The Ambassadors', p. 125, reproduced by courtesy of the Trustees, National Gallery, London; Robert Hunt Library/Imperial War Museum, p. 141.

CONTENTS

UNIT	TITLE	PAGE	STRUCTURES	FUNCTIONS
1	Joining	5	Non-defining relatives Participle constructions, e.g. . . . *bringing* the total to; *boosted* by . . . Apposition	Defining Comparing Enumerating
2	Contrasts	24	Comparatives Concessive may and might Structures with although, even though, despite, in spite of, nevertheless, whereas, unlike, even if, rather than, yet	Contrasting Defining Disarming
3	Logical relations	38	Conditionals Modal verbs – should, ought, must, need, could, might, will Verb patterns – mean, involve, prevent, necessitate, aim, intend Present and past participles	Expressing cause, effect and influence Deducing Challenging assumptions Expressing tentativeness
4	Omission	57	Passives (with and without 'get') Passive gerund If only and past perfect Wish (to express regret)	Comparing past and present Expressing regret Avoiding responsibility Defining failings
5	The general and the particular	73	Modals – should, ought, must (to describe duties, rights) supposed to Particularisers, e.g. primarily, chiefly, specifically Irregular plurals, plurals of compounds and foreign words	Generalising Disagreeing with generalisations Focusing attention Advising Justifying

UNIT	TITLE	PAGE	STRUCTURES	FUNCTIONS
6	Standpoint	89	Modals – might, should, could, need (to express criticism etc.) Were to have (done) Supposed to have (done) Wish	Making invitations, requests and enquiries in appropriate language Defining beliefs and prejudices Expressing irritation and disapproval Criticising
7	In the negative	108	Modals in past – should, might, could, must have (done) 'Problem' negatives, e.g. we think so too – we don't think so either; I'd rather – not: you'd better – you'd better not	Adducing causes Responding negatively to requests Apologising Dissuading
8	Emphasis	124	Cleft and pseudo-cleft Sentences, e.g. It's money we need; What we need is money. Inversion of subject and verb Emphasisers, intensifiers and maximisers	Emphasising Reassuring Responding enthusiastically
9	In the mind	138	Past continuous (narrative) As if . . . Verb patterns: deduce, conclude, imply, assume, realise, imagine	Expressing connotations Defining Pre-invitations Expressing responses to poetry
10	Not quite clear	151	Ambiguity Future continuous Verb patterns: assume, expect, forget, realise	Asking for clarification Expressing possibility and doubt Requesting elaboration Defining

Units 1–10, Text B
Alphabetical index of topics, functions and grammar points

INTRODUCTION

WHO IS *PROSPECTS* FOR?

Prospects is for advanced learners of English who wish to make real progress with their reading, listening and writing skills and, more particularly, to develop their active vocabulary, fluency and structural accuracy to the point where they are able to control the forms and lexis of English with confidence and precision.

HOW IS THE BOOK ORGANISED?

The book consists of ten units, each of which is built round a linguistically and educationally productive concept (e.g. 'joining', 'logical relations', 'the general and the particular').

HOW IS EACH UNIT ORGANISED?

Each consists of six main elements: reading passages (two for each unit: Text A in unit, Text B at end of book), communicative activities, listening activities, structure and usage exercises, writing activities and study notes. Each of these elements is closely linked to the overall concept treated in the unit.

WHAT METHOD DOES THE BOOK EMPLOY?

Prospects seeks to combine the best of communicative teaching with a concern for structural accuracy.

The authors of *Prospects* believe in controlled discussion preceded by preparation. Students are told that they will be asked to give their opinions, talk about their experience, or say what they know about a serious topic of wide interest. They then study the language in which to formulate their response before practising it in pairs or very small groups. Finally, they compare their responses with those of all the other students and practise their interactional skills by taking part in a discussion involving the whole group.

HOW IS LISTENING TREATED?

Listening is a skill which can be developed (students studying this book have already become fluent and therefore have already learned to listen).

Prospects allows students to use and extend their skills in natural activities and discussion, by taking part in a variety of activities introduced by and dependent on their listening skills. These activities test understanding and develop confidence; they encourage communication in the fullest sense. They will also help students to avoid selectively hearing only what they want to, reporting vague impressions as facts and manufacturing evidence to support them.

AND PRONUNCIATION?

Apart from the models to be found in the tapescript, it ought to be emphasised that the pronunciation of words should always be studied when their meanings are looked up in a dictionary.

Cambridge 1988   John Percil
London 1988   Joanna Gray

Key to symbols

 work in pairs

 work as a group

 this is recorded on cassette

1 JOINING

Relationships, groups and organisations; achieving compromises

A READING TEXTS

1 READING

a Group A read Text A. Group B read Text B (on page 169).

b Group A tell Group B what Text A is about, remembering the main points in the text. Group B ask Group A questions about Text A until they have a good idea of the content.

c Do the same with Text B. Group B tell Group A what Text B is about, remembering the characteristics of the 'stages' referred to. Group A ask Group B questions about Text B.

d Groups A and B read each other's texts.

Text A

MARRIAGE

Marriage, it's commonly said, is a toss-up – there's no way of telling which way it will go until you've got married.

But that's just one of the widely-held views of marriage that current thinking has disproved. Over the last ten years there have been endless hours of research, a huge number of surveys and mountains of books written on the subject. But the same seven factors crop up time again in the most successful marriage partnerships. It follows, then, that the more of those factors you and your partner can claim to have, the more likely your marriage is to be happy and successful.

To check how these factors figure in your marriage, look at Ex. B.1, Communicative activities [on page 7]. If you don't have many of the factors working in your favour there's no need to write your marriage off. Knowing where the problem might be is half the battle.

For example, one important factor is that you agree about finances and lifestyle: but if in practice you spend most of the time arguing over these things, don't despair: it's the ability to compromise rather than the ability to agree on every issue that influences marital happiness.

Knowing which marriage myths have been proved – or disproved – by research can also help you see your partnership more clearly. As we might expect, all the evidence shows that we tend to choose a partner from within a loose group of friends, neighbours or colleagues. When it actually comes to making a choice, statistics show it's best to choose a partner whom you admire and trust for personal characteristics like warmth, generosity and enthusiastic attitude to life, since it is on these intimate qualities that the development and stability of your marriage will depend and grow. Those who marry for status or money usually find later that their partner's intimate qualities do not match their exterior circumstances, and those who marry in a wave of romance and little else are less likely to have a successful relationship too, since the romance fades.

The age at which you marry affects your chances of a happy marriage too. A quarter of all teenage brides are divorced within the first ten years of marriage and almost half of them are divorced before they reach their silver wedding.

Perhaps surprisingly, the theory that living together before marriage improves your chances of marital success is not borne out by research. Once a couple marry, the fact that they lived together first makes little difference.

And the idea that opposites attract has also been disproved. A number of surveys have shown that while there are some successful relationships of complementary nature (where one partner makes up for what the other lacks), statistically these have fewer chances of success than marriages where the partners are alike. It is not just similarity of interests which counts here but similarity of family background, age, education, expectations of marriage and ability to express yourself emotionally. Our ideas of family life are often based on what our parents' marriage was like. We may try to emulate it or to live in a totally different style, depending on whether we enjoyed or rejected our childhood. Sometimes people deliberately choose partners who are totally unlike their original family (perhaps from different countries and cultures), but find their feelings change as a result of marriage itself and they end up by rejecting the 'different' partner for the same reasons that they were once attracted to them. Problems can also occur when one partner grows out of the couple's familiar background and wants to leave it while the other is not yet ready to go.

Living magazine

 2 QUESTIONS ON THE TEXTS

TEXT A

Think of the type of publication in which you might see this article and also of the kind of reader it is aimed at. Make suggestions, giving your reasons based on evidence in the text.

TEXT B

a   As for Text A, suggest the type of publication that would carry this kind of article and point to evidence in the text. Is it aimed at a different kind of reader from Text A?

b   Does your experience of friendship accord with this description? Have you five or six real friends?

B COMMUNICATIVE ACTIVITIES

1 MARRIAGE (see Study Notes, page 21)

The magazine from which Text A was taken also gives seven pointers to a successful marriage:

a There must be mutual respect and admiration.

b You agree about finances and lifestyle.

c You can talk to each other openly about anything.

d You have similar personalities, are of similar age and share the same background and religion.

e There must be flexibility on both sides regarding domestic and career roles.

f You delay having a family until you've been married several years.

g You are good friends as well as lovers.

    i   Go through the pointers a–g and discuss what each involves.

    ii   Choose the *two* pointers that in your opinion are the most important and then say *why* you consider them important.

    iii Choose the one you *disagree* with most and say why.

    iv Would you like to add any more? Discuss with the group.

    v   What might be the particular problems for couples getting married if they are (a) teenagers (b) in their sixties (c) a West Indian and English (mixed) couple?

2 FRIENDS (see Study Notes, page 21)

Have you got a very wide circle of friends? Are you particularly good at maintaining friendships or really rather bad? Social psychologists have now isolated specific friendship skills at which some people are more adept than others. These skills are especially related to reciprocity and behaviour with third parties and some of them are listed below.

a Always show emotional support.

b Don't just share your successes – tell him or her about your failures too!

c Accept him or her as he or she is.

d Be a good listener.

e Respect each other's privacy.

    i   Explain what (a), (c) and (d) might involve.

    ii With regard to (e), 'Respect each other's privacy', where would you draw the line between what is shared and what is private in (a) a close friendship (b) a marriage?

TALKING ABOUT FRIENDSHIP

iii Somebody once said that a friend is someone you can wake up in the middle of the night to borrow £25 and a raincoat. What would your definition be?

iv To what extent is it possible to have real friends (without a sexual element) of the opposite sex?

v Say how the following relate to the subject of friendship:
possessiveness   'give and take'
confidences   'a shoulder to cry on'

vi Are there essential differences between male/male and female/female friendships?

vii 'Drink deep but not always of the same cup', a poet said of close relationships. What did he mean?

3 GROUPS

At some stage in their lives most people belong to a social group of some description. It may be an extremely loose and informal grouping of old school-friends, professional colleagues, or just like-minded people who perhaps meet for leisure or general social purposes or, at the other extreme, the highly formalised structure of the religious organisation or the political party.

a Give examples of:
  i   professional groups
  ii ideological groups
  iii leisure or interest groups

b The following are the aims, in very general terms, of certain organisations. protest groups etc. First identify the organisations concerned and then discuss in which ways those groups set about achieving their objectives. (There are sometimes several possibilities.)

  i   To represent the interests of workers in negotiations over pay and conditions. To offer any advice, legal aid or financial support needed in disputes with employers.

  ii To encourage boys to become responsible and self-reliant members of society by giving them practical expertise and developing leadership skills.

  iii To provide 'neutral' medical care for the casualties of war and, in peace time, to provide emergency relief for the victims of natural disasters.

  iv To make large sums of money illegally by means of secret criminal organisations especially in Sicily, the rest of Italy and the USA.

  v   To obtain information about the military and economic capabilities and the political intentions of another country.

  vi To act as a watchdog in matters of design, quality, price and service and to represent the interests of the public in their dealings with commercial enterprises.

  vii To try to destroy the stockpile of nuclear weapons in the world and stop further production of them.

c   Think of a group or organisation that you belong to or once were a member of and answer the following questions:

i   What were the qualifications for membership?

ii   What were the aims and activities of the group?

iii Were there any characteristics of social background, dress or language that linked its members?

iv   What is/was the ethos of the group? (= their characteristic guiding beliefs, the shared attitudes and spiritual values).

v   What are the human qualities that are/were necessary to be a good member of the group?

vi   To what extent did individual preferences and wishes have to be sacrificed to the wider interest of the group?

vii Did/Do you ever find yourself at variance with the group as a whole? In what way?

4 MAKING COMPROMISES

Whether in relationships, professional life or in the wider sphere of national politics and international diplomacy, situations frequently occur where a compromise of some sort has to be negotiated between two or more conflicting interests. Look at the following examples of negotiating positions and discuss possible compromises between the two sides that might resolve the problem and suggest what actual language might be used to propose the compromise, taking care to adjust the language to the different situations.

Position A	Possible compromise	Position B
Example: Deborah prefers German white wine and dislikes all red wine.	*How about some French white wine? In that case let's have some rosé, shall we?*	Jim likes most wines but prefers red wine. He does not like German wine very much.
a Manufacturer asks for £500 per 1000 items.		Buyer offers £350 per 1000 and asks for 12% discount on orders over 5000.
b Tom wants to go to sleep immediately and can't sleep if the light or radio is on.		His wife doesn't feel very sleepy and wants to read or listen to the radio.
c The production manager wants to employ twenty new production workers immediately.		The Financial Director has stopped all new staff appointments for six months.
d Susan's mother insists on buying all Susan's clothes for her until she is at least 15.		Susan (12) wants to start buying all her own clothes now (with her mother's money).
e Superpower A will agree to monthly aerial inspection of troop movements only if this is done in its *own* planes.		Superpower B wants to use *its* plane when inspecting Superpower A's troop dispositions and would prefer the overflights to be at two-week intervals.
f Karl thinks he should be able to read his wife's diary if he wants to. On the other hand, he doesn't like her reading all his letters.		His wife prefers to keep her diary locked. It's her personal space, she says. Yet she feels she should be allowed to read her husband's letters ('letters are different').

SUGGESTING COMPROMISES

5 APHORISMS AND SAYINGS ABOUT LOVE

Of course through the ages so much has been said about love. Here are some provocative examples, mainly from famous literary figures.

a   Read through them and think about their exact meaning.

   i   In love, there is always one who kisses and one who offers the cheek. (*French proverb*)
   ii   Love does not dominate; it cultivates. (*Johann Wolfgang von Goethe*)
   iii True love is like seeing ghosts: we all talk about it, but few of us have ever seen one. (*Duc François de La Rochefoucauld*)
   iv   No disguise can long conceal love where it exists, or long feign it where it is lacking. (*Duc François de La Rochefoucauld*)
   v   Woman inspires us to great things, and prevents us from achieving them. (*Alexandre Dumas*)
   vi   At the beginning of love and at its end the lovers are embarrassed to be left alone. (*Jean de La Bruyère*)
   vii Love begins with love; friendship, however warm, cannot change to love, however mild. (*Jean de La Bruyère*)
   viii Love does not consist in gazing at each other but in looking together in the same direction. (*Antoine de Saint-Exupéry*)

b   Choose one of the above and, when you are ready, tell the rest of the group in your own words what you think it means.

c   Discuss the answers to the following questions on the sayings. The number of each question refers to the number of the proverb or saying.

   i   Is it impossible to have a relationship where both people offer the cheek and both kiss equally?
   ii   How do people try to dominate their loved one and what are the forms that 'cultivation' might take?
   iii By his choice of simile ('ghosts'), is the author really saying that there is no such thing as true love or merely that it is extremely rare?
   iv   How does our love for somebody show despite our efforts to conceal it?
   v   Doesn't it all depend on what we mean by 'great things'? Perhaps men and women have totally different definitions?
   vi   Always?
   vii Never?
   viii Why can't love be simply a matter of gazing at each other?

1

6 THE —— THAT'S GOT EVERYTHING

Advertisements, publicity handouts, brochures etc. often include the following types of sayings:

Bank with the Midland, *the listening bank*!
Come to the Isle of Wight, *the jewel of the South*.
Bring the family to Alton Towers, *the theme park that's got everything*!

a   How would you complete the following in a similar way?

   i   Come to Paris, ...
   ii   Choose American Express, ...
   iii This year spend some time in Scotland, ...
   iv   Your cat deserves Kit-e-Kat, ...
   v   Make it Zermatt this winter, ...
   vi   Fly Air France, ...
   vii Choose Ford, ...
   viii Indulge yourself at the Sheraton, ...
   ix   Say it with flowers, ...
   x   Take *The Times*, ...

b   Suggest two examples of your own.

7 TWO-PART ADVERTISEMENTS AND SLOGANS

a

Choose Intasun
Why pay more?

b

HOOVER.
WHO BETTER?

APPOSITION

c

diet Coca-Cola Great taste. One calorie **diet Coke**

d

Sealink
Lots more.

e

NUCLEAR STATE   POLICE STATE

All these advertisements or slogans consist of two parts which are mostly separated by a full stop on the page but which we combine into one sentence when we read them. Discuss how you could express each in one complete sentence. There is usually more than one possibility.

C LISTENING ACTIVITIES

You have become a member of a new group, a group of students with similar objectives. Groups have been identified as having certain peculiarities: they

STORM	– feel uncomfortable, argue, size up other members
NORM	– feel more secure, discuss
CONFORM	– decide on acceptable behaviour and procedures
PERFORM	– follow these procedures in order to achieve objectives (Performing involves communication, sharing ideas, seeking answers and doing it all as a part of a group.)

INTERPRETING AND LINKING

 1 Now form groups. Study the photographs of the two bottles. Your objectives are to offer free ideas as to how the bottles were filled. Ground rules will be given by your teacher. There will be time for discussion after this activity.

2 Listen to the first recorded problem. Then work in your original group to reach a decision on these questions:

a Do you consider Henry Addams' behaviour to be unusual?
b If so, in what way?
c How do you think his colleagues felt about him?
d Why did he behave in this way?

3 Here is another chance to practise your group skills. Listen to another recorded problem and feel free to offer any sensible solutions.

D STRUCTURE AND LANGUAGE USAGE

1 JOINING SENTENCES (see Study Notes, page 22)

Make a new sentence of the following, integrating the extra information into the existing sentence by means of a relative with or without a preposition, an *-ing* form, etc. When integrating the new information into a bare sentence you will want to use a range of forms. Integrate the following, as in the example:

Example: Boston is the capital of Massachusetts, USA.
i   It's a major financial centre.
ii It was founded in 1630.
  = *Boston, a major financial centre, is the capital of Massachusetts./Boston, which was founded in 1630, is the capital of Massachusetts.*

a   Henry Moore died in 1986 at the age of 88.
  i   world-famous sculptor
  ii   He was influenced by primitive African and Mexican art.
  iii There were no British sculptors of comparable stature before him.

b   Aberdeen has in recent years become an important service centre for the North Sea oilfields.
  i   It is situated between the mouths of the Rivers Don and Dee.
  ii   It has a population of 200,000.
  iii Some important research institutes have been established there.

c   The Bank of England was founded in 1694.
  i   Its nickname is 'The Old Lady of Threadneedle Street'.
  ii   It was a private institution before 1946.
  iii Its main function is to act as a central bank.

d   Ten new oil-fired power stations are being built.
  i   Three of them are almost finished.
  ii   This will bring the total up to 53.
  iii Most of them are located in the north of the country.

e   Bertrand Russell was one of the greatest philosophers of his time.
  i   author of *Principia Mathematica*
  ii   He was imprisoned for his pacifism in 1918.
  iii He was awarded the Nobel Prize for literature in 1950.

f   Consumer spending is expected to remain at record levels in the coming months.
  i   It is boosted by strong growth in real incomes.
  ii   particularly spending on consumer durables

g   Nobody seemed to notice Celia's engagement ring or her new dress.
  i   This annoyed her.
  ii They talked about her brother's car and his recent promotion. (Use *instead*.)

h   Concorde came into service in 1976.
  i   It was built by the French and British.
  ii The cost was borne by French and British taxpayers.
  iii Only twenty were built.

2 THE VOCABULARY OF JOINING (see Study Notes, page 23)

an alliance	a fusion	an alloy
to link	a synthesis	a compound
to amalgamate	unification	a coalition
a union	to bring together	to merge/a merger
a federation	a blend/to blend	

Match each of the items in the box with a sentence below and then make a new sentence of approximately the same meaning, using the word from the box and making any necessary changes. (Sometimes there is more than one possibility and an idea may be used more than once.)

Example:
With effect from 1st September, the functions of Sales Manager and Advertising Manager will be performed by a new Marketing Manager.
= *With effect from 1st September, the functions of Sales Manager and Advertising Manager will be amalgamated/brought together in the new post of Marketing Manager.*

a   Every year they attend a special blessing in church, to give thanks for their marriage.

b   It's difficult to describe their music accurately – I suppose they've been strongly influenced by blues and Brazilian music.

c   She made it to the top because she had courage mixed with amazing determination.

d   After a weekend of intense political speculation the three main parties agreed to work together to form a government.

e   The word 'playboy' is made up of the words 'play' and 'boy'.

f   There are twice-weekly air services from the mainland to the island, and a monthly ferry.

g   There's a club in most larger cities, so now they've decided to come together in a national organisation with offices in London.

h In many ways it's entirely logical that they should join forces. In product range, market share and turnover they're closely comparable.

i Cavour worked to make Italy into one country.

j The broad aim of the conference was that experts working in the same technical area should meet to exchange expertise.

k In his present work he's trying to bring together several prominent themes of his previous work into a new whole.

l In view of the growing threat from larger neighbours, these three countries quickly decided on military cooperation in case of war.

m Their wine has been carefully mixed with wine from other areas to produce a smoother taste.

n Aluminium bronze is produced by fusing aluminium with copper.

3 MAKING COMPOUNDS

Technical, business, scientific English as well as newspaper-style make great use of two and three part 'compounds' made from two, three, or even four nouns:-

noun 1   noun 2   noun 3
Holiday   disaster   jet was fit to fly.

noun 1   noun 2   noun 1a   noun 2a   noun 3a
Community   ministers in   *terrorism   crisis   talks.*

        noun 1   noun 2   noun 3   noun 4
The   *laser   scalpel   light   source* is an innovation . . .!
(*Scientific report on a new kind of scalpel for surgeons*)

a Look at Text A in Unit 10 (Computer software for working with language) and collect four or five examples of these 'compounds' (usually made from *two* nouns).

b Look at the following sentences and then shorten them by using the nouns in a 'compound' of at least *three* nouns:

Example: Firms in Britain's sunrise industries are facing a dilemma.
= Britain's *sunrise industry firms* are facing a dilemma.

    i   The cost of fuel for road haulage is still rising. (Put 'cost' into the plural). Road . . .

    ii   Manufacturers of textiles for the fashion trade are experiencing difficult market conditions. Fashion . . .

    iii The figures for unemployment for July show a slight rise on June.

    iv   The consumption of electricity during the daytime has risen by 65% since 1986.

v   Forecasts on inflation issued by the government in recent years have been consistently wrong.
vi High street spending in August tops £7 billion.
vii The reorganisation of ICI in 1985–6 is now beginning to bear fruit.
viii Courses offered by the Open University in computer technology have doubled in number in only two years.

E WRITING ACTIVITIES

1

The following is the remainder of Text A from which some of the language (including verbs) has been omitted. Join the items up into three paragraphs, supplying suitable vocabulary where necessary and putting the verbs in brackets into an appropriate form.

Married for ten years, during which time Paul's income had expanded, Jessica had only recently/back to work after/two children. Their relationship/always/stormy one but it/never/boring. However, as Paul's authority/power grew/work, so/his desire/get his own way/home, (make)/relationship/stormier at a time/Jessica (try)/cope/new job as well as/care of/children. Jessica's feelings/opinions (treat)/scant respect/she responded/a series/short-term affairs/men/met/work.

The crisis came when Paul insisted on moving into a very expensive home in an exclusive district. Jessica didn't want/move/her opinion/ignored. Without/sense/support/gained from her former neighbours/local friends/she decided/wasn't/point left/marriage/couple eventually split up.

Jessica and Paul's marriage failed because Paul refused to take his wife's feelings and anxieties seriously. He/incapable/(resolve) tricky issues except/insisting/his own way/although Jessica constantly asked him, he refused/talk through/marriage problems/counsellor. Unfortunately, Jessica wasn't/persistent, (prefer)/take/easy way out/necessary confrontations by (turn) to/series/short-term lovers instead. If the couple (talk)/counsellor,/strong feelings for each other (can) (channel into) (make)/marriage work.

2 PREFIXES (see Study Notes, page 23)

a   Complete the table below with appropriate prefixes and give three examples of each.

b   Write a sentence of your own, using each prefix.

Prefix	Meaning	Examples
Example *UN-*	to reverse a process (added to verbs)	*unpack* *unsettle* *unlock*
i	do something better, longer etc. than	....
ii	against, in opposition to (added to verbs and abstract nouns)	....
iii	badly, bad (added to verbs, abstract nouns, adjectives)	....
iv	wrongly, in error (added to verbs, abstract nouns)	....
v	extremely, excessively (added to adjectives)	....
vi	joint, accompanying (added to verbs and nouns)	....
vii	too much (added to verbs and adjectives)	....
viii	before (added to verbs and abstract nouns)	....
ix	between, among (added to adjectives, verbs and nouns)	....

STUDY NOTES

B1 MARRIAGE

Useful language for discussion

i have respect for; the kind of person you can respect; like the same things; similar tastes; similar attitudes to money; not to be able to talk; to keep things to yourself; to talk something through (e.g. a problem); to talk about what's bothering you; to have the same attitudes to things; to see things in the same way; to help with the house; to share/the household chores/in running the house; a 'house-husband'; to wait 'until you're sure'; to provide a good home for.

ii In my opinion the two most important are . . .; I think the main two are . . .; My two would be . . . .

B2 FRIENDS

Useful vocabulary for discussion

i (a) to need cheering up; to give advice; to be on hand when needed
 (c) to criticise; to try to change someone; tolerant; easy-going
 (d) to help somebody to solve their problems; to talk through a problem; someone to talk to

ii I would draw the line at (reading my wife's diary); I think it's going too far to read each other's letters; I would never . . .; I wouldn't think of . . .; I think if you're married you should . . .; Everyone needs their own personal space; 'room to breathe'; trust (n and v); to have your own friends (marriage).

iii My idea/conception of a friend is . . .; For me a friend is . . .; I suppose for me a friend is someone . . . .

iv a platonic relationship; perfectly possible; some of my best friends are . .; a sexual element

v being clinging (colloquial)/jealous; wanting someone to yourself; being flexible; to take the rough with the smooth; to confide in somebody; to keep a secret; to discuss one's innermost problems

vi to talk openly; to keep one's feelings 'bottled up' (= repressed); to reveal your feelings to somebody

vii to have experiences on your own account; your own circle of friends; develop your own interests

1 STUDY NOTES

B3 GROUPS

Useful language for discussion

b to take up a case (e.g. of injustice to an employee); to put pressure on; to strike; to negotiate working conditions; to give somebody responsibility; adventure training; self-reliance; respect for nature; comradeship; camps; to put somebody in charge of (others); to tend the wounded; to give first aid; to transport medical supplies; give medical assistance; provide nursing personnel; corrupt officials; to push drugs; to demand ransoms; kidnap; blackmail; protection rackets; to spy; to 'bug' premises; to tap telephone calls; directional microphones; monitoring (listening to radio broadcasts); to carry out tests on e.g. appliances; to take up a complaint against a retailer/manufacturer; to make representations to government on consumer affairs; to hold protest marches; to campaign; to get publicity; to make people more generally aware of . . .; to put the other side of the argument

B5 APHORISMS AND SAYINGS ABOUT LOVE

Useful language for discussion

c manipulate; keep in a cage; allow to grow; develop in new directions; exist; a delusion; an illusion; obvious to everybody; an inspiration to achievement; make demands on them; to have so much to say to each other; to have nothing to say to each other; platonic; depends how it starts; looking outwards/inwards; obsessed; inward-looking

D1 JOINING SENTENCES

Study the following examples and use the information they provide on structure to help you complete D1.

Example: Thomas Edison made the first electric light bulb.
- i the inventor
- ii Some people consider him the most prolific inventor of all time.
- iii His research laboratory was situated in Menlo Park, New Jersey.
- i Thomas Edison, *the inventor*, made the first electric light bulb.
- ii Thomas Edison, *who some people consider to be the most prolific inventor of all time* . . .
- iii Thomas Edison, *whose research laboratory was situated in Menlo Park, New Jersey*, made the first . . .

Example: Ottawa is the capital of Canada.
- i It is in south-east Ontario.
- ii It was founded in the early nineteenth century.
- i Ottawa, *which is in south-east Ontario*, is the capital of Canada.
- ii Ottawa, *which was founded in the early nineteenth century*, is the capital of Canada.

Example: A woman of 72 passed her English 'O' level this summer.
- i It surprised her friends.
- ii Her husband said she was crazy to try.
- i A woman of 72 passed her English 'O' level this summer, *which surprised her friends*.
- ii A woman of 72, *whose husband said she was crazy to try*, passed her 'O' level this summer.

D2 THE VOCABULARY OF JOINING

Before attempting D2, check that you know not only the meanings of the following but also how they are typically used and pronounced.
a federation, a union, unification, an alliance, a fusion, an alloy, a compound, a coalition, to merge, a merger, to bring together, to blend, a blend, a synthesis, to amalgamate, to link, to synthesise.

E WRITING ACTIVITIES

2 PREFIXES

hypersensitive   **mal**treat   **inter**marriage
prefabricate   **co**existence   **mis**lay
to **over**simplify   **anti**freeze   **un**do
counteract   **out**class   **fore**sight

Find out the meanings of the words above and in particular what part the prefix plays in the meaning. For example, a 'pseudonym' is a false name. The prefix 'pseudo' carries the meaning of 'false'. Another example would be 'pseudoscientific' meaning 'pretending to be scientific'.

STUDY NOTES 1

2 CONTRASTS

Making comparisons; talking about differences

A READING TEXTS

1 READING

See Unit 1, Section A (page 5) for instructions. Text B for this unit will be found on page 170.

Text A

THE LESSON WE REFUSE TO LEARN
by Royce Logan Turner

It is the end of term. Every time I look out of the window or step out of the door I can see the BMW, or the Jaguar, or the Volvo, coming to pick up Emma, or Daphne, or Amanda, or Robert, or Daniel.

The students being collected are, for the most part, obviously young, but also healthy, slim and well-dressed. And most of them appear to be happy. It is daddy, of course, who has seen to it that they have lots of nice, brightly coloured clothes; a good holiday abroad; enough money for social events – the balls and the bars. They even see to it that some of the students have cars.

I began to think of my own adolescence and young adulthood as I watched the BMWs pull in, and to contrast it with theirs. I began also to think of my contemporaries in Barnsley, with whom I had shared part of that young adulthood, and to think of their lives and futures, which provided an even more stark contrast. On reflection what is most striking is the inordinately different level of wealth, and of opportunity; the inordinately different starting points in life. It has never been clearer to me than now just how much some people have to struggle against all kinds of adversity – financial, social, against disrespect, accorded to certain regional accents – whilst others are handed opportunities on a plate.

I have been living with students this year in a university residential block, and a roll-call of fathers' professions in there would include: medical doctor; lawyer; tax accountant; affluent businessman; university professor; and the list goes on. At least in this block, and I am sure this is replicated elsewhere, there is a decided absence of the children of miners, shop-workers, dockers, bus drivers.

I do not begrudge all this. For those benefiting, it is a glamorous and quite exciting existence, and if I had had the same kind of background I would have made the most of it. But it does focus one's attention on the gross inequality of wealth in this country and the concomitant inequality of opportunities. I am beginning to think the latter is more of an evil than the former because it means, first of all, that there are vast numbers of people who never develop to their full potential; and, secondly, as a result, the country is wasting and misallocating on a huge scale intelligence and labour-power resources.

It simply cannot be true that young working-class people are inherently thicker than their middle-class counterparts. Or am I wrong? As a nation have we come to accept that they are? As far as education policy goes, it certainly seems – from my observations of how it actually works out on the ground – that we probably have. And the extent of the inequality of opportunity facing young adults is, of course, compounded by the fact that these middle-class youngsters also benefit from their families' accretion of directional guidance. In other words, families of this sort will guide their sons and daughters into certain lucrative professions; or inculcate upon them an appreciation of the value of entrepreneurial zest; or provide them with contacts for good jobs. All the sort of things which are absent in ordinary, working class homes, where there is much less idea how one gains entry to professions; often no direct experience of higher education; little 'feel' for entrepreneurship, as the predominant means of earning a living has always been to sell one's labour to someone else.

Of course, not everyone at university conforms with the description I have outlined. There are those from less advantaged families, those struggling to make ends meet, and those relying on the goodwill of the bank manager to get by. But it remains a fact that there is a disproportionate number of young adults at university who are as I have described them. And that is no slur on them, or their families; but it is a truth and a clearly observable one. At university, one can see in its full glory a middle-class elite perpetuating itself and consolidating its socially elevated position.

Social divisions in this country are now so great as to be positively unhealthy and destabilising, which must be a worry even to those who seek a perpetuation of the economic and political status quo. Acceptance of the need for change in education – especially higher education – and in the distribution of wealth and opportunities is long overdue. Some way has to be found to bring about a more balanced spread of people at university; and some way has to be found to extend opportunities.

If society fails to do this, it is both depriving itself of economic resources and, by frustrating people's chances of fulfilling their potential, storing up trouble for the future. Unless such changes are effected, the consequences do not bear thinking about. The lid cannot be kept on the volcano forever. Eventually, those in the regions of despair will recognise what is happening elsewhere and begin to resent the beneficiaries of the affluent world. Unless things change, we shall see an ever greater increase of crime, met by an increasingly heavily armed police force; we shall see towns and cities turn into unliveable ghettos; we shall see a middle class clinging desperately to its material wealth in a sea of despair.

The Guardian 14 July 1986

2 QUESTIONS ON THE TEXTS

TEXT A

a Does the author give a balanced account of the problem, in your opinion?

b What is 'the lesson we refuse to learn'?

c Would you say it is a very intelligent analysis?

TEXT B

At the end of the fourth paragraph John Holt hints that the *teacher* is responsible for the desire on the part of some pupils for only one answer. Do you agree?

BOTH TEXTS

'The authors of both texts are wasting their time fussing and complaining about innate differences between human beings.' Do you agree?

B COMMUNICATIVE ACTIVITIES

 1 CLASS CONSCIOUSNESS (see Study Notes, page 36)

The British are obsessed by class, a social commentator has said, unlike the Germans and Americans, who are obsessed by money.

In the 1960s and early 1970s in the UK classlessness became fashionable, class barriers started coming down, and young people with 'posh'* upper-class accents went downmarket and tried to sound like people lower down the social scale. Now, however, the UK has returned to normal, and is just as class conscious as it was thirty years ago. 'If you've got it (= class), flaunt it (= display it)' people say now.

a How has the class system in your country changed over the last 80 years? Are people very class conscious now?

b The following factors are crucial in classifying people:
Birth and social background
The way people speak (accent and vocabulary)
Education (Boarding-school? Oxbridge?)
Financial resources
Where you live (castle or council flat?)
Dress
Pick out those that are important in your country and add different criteria if necessary. Explain them to someone who does not know your country; go into as much detail as possible. Rank them in order of importance.

---

* 'posh': 60 years ago more fashionable passengers used to travel on the *p*ort side *o*ut from Britain to India and in a *s*tarboard cabin on the voyage *h*ome.

c   Say how the following relate to class:
   i   status symbols   v   the newly rich
   ii   a meritocracy   vi   them-and-us attitudes
   iii snobs   vii   deference
   iv   social mobility   viii a chip on your shoulder

d   How easy is it to move up the social scale in your country? How do people show that they are moving up?

MAKING COMPARISONS

e   What is your attitude to class systems? Do you see them as:
    i   a strange relic from a bygone age?
    ii   an inevitable and permanent feature of social life?
    iii harmless fun?
    iv   dangerous nonsense?
         Why?
f   Is it possible to have a classless society?
g   So which class are *you*? Or do you consider yourself classless?

'Good. We're middle class!'

2 CONTRASTS IN INTELLIGENCE (see Study Notes, page 36)

a   Recalling Text B, give John Holt's views and complete the table.

	'Intelligent'	**'Dull'**
i	Eager to get into contact with reality	More inclined to live in world of fantasy
ii	....	Much less interested in what is going on around him/her
iii	Tackles new situations boldly, experiments	....
iv	....	Gives up if he/she makes mistakes
v	Patiently endures uncertainty and failure	....
vi	....	Unwilling to proceed until he/she is sure of the way ahead
vii	Feels the universe is on the whole a reasonable and trustworthy place	....

HOW CLASS IS DEFINED

b Do you agree with the ideas expressed here?

c Discuss how you would define the following terms, taking care to bring out the differences between them:

i	a good brain	v	a trained mind
ii	genius	vi	understanding
iii	cleverness	vii	wisdom
iv	insight	viii	common sense

 d Which of the above are closely related to:

i	ability to do a crossword	iv	business acumen
ii	feelings	v	imagination
iii	academic ability	vi	skill in human relationships

 e Describe the kind of intelligence that each of the following might possess:

i	a great engineer	v	a great statesman
ii	a great novelist	vi	a great sportsman
iii	a self-made multi-millionaire	vii	a great religious figure
iv	a great painter		

 f What in your opinion is the typical attitude of intelligent people (your own definition) to the following:

i other races and cultures
ii their own mistakes and failures in professional and personal life
iii money
iv war

 g How would you characterise *your own* kind of intelligence? For example, is it extremely orderly and analytical or wild and imaginative?

3 PAST AND PRESENT (see Study Notes, page 36)

 A CONTRASTS BETWEEN EXAMINATIONS 1936–86

The following represent extracts from examinations for official administrative positions in the UK. The first is similar to one set in 1936, the second is similar to one set 50 years later. Study both texts carefully and then answer the questions below.

1936
Time allowed: 1 hour.

1   Read the following poem and then answer questions (a), (b) and (c).
>Of Nelson and the North
> Sing the glorious day's renown,
>When the battle fierce came forth
> All the might of Denmark's crown . . .

a   Relate in your own words the story in this poem.

b   Explain these phrases: Sing the glorious day's renown; All the might of Denmark's crown.

c   Comment on the metre and rhyme scheme of this poem.

2   Explain the following figures of speech and give an example of each: metaphor, onomatopoeia; climax; oxymoron; antithesis.

1986

1   Data sufficiency test
Jane lives in one of the houses in a terrace of three, which is separated by wide gaps from any other houses. The three houses in the terrace differ from one another in plan. They are numbered 1, 2 and 3 in order. Which ONE piece of information do you need to identify the one in which Jane lives?

a   Jane has one reception room and three bedrooms.

b   Numbers 1 and 2 have one reception room.

c   Numbers 2 and 3 each have three bedrooms.

d   When working in her garden, Jane is often annoyed by the smoke of her neighbours' bonfires.

e   Jane can hear her neighbours' record players clearly through the walls on both sides.

2   Identify the pattern and determine how many dots there should be in each half of the domino with a dotted outline.

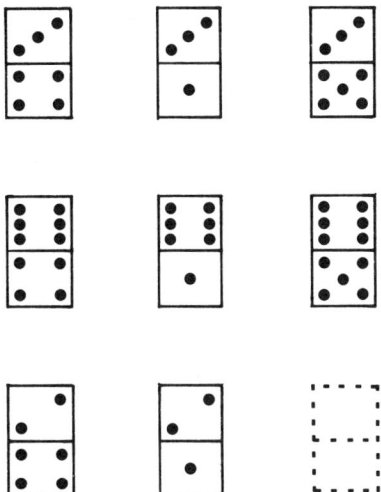

Questions about the tests

i   What different skills do the two tests examine?

ii How do you account for the striking contrast between the two exams?

iii Can you relate the contrast to (a) cultural change and (b) changes in work conditions and procedures?

iv What are the answers to the first two questions in the 1986 test?

B WORKING CONDITIONS 1854–1986

This is a notice to shop assistants from 1854. Contrast the rules with present-day conditions and discuss which rules you would find particularly onerous:

> Store must open promptly at 6 a.m. until 9 p.m. all the year round.
> Store must be swept, counter, base shelves and showcases dusted. Lamps trimmed, filled and chimney cleaned, pens made, doors and windows opened.
> A pail of water and scuttle of coal must be brought in by each clerk before breakfast, if there is time to do so and attend customers who call.
> Any employee who is in the habit of smoking Spanish cigars, getting shaved at a barber's shop, going to dances, and other such places of amusement will surely give his employer reason to be suspicious of his integrity and all round honesty.
> Each employee must pay not less than one guinea per year to the church and attend Sunday School every Sunday.
> Men are given one evening a week for courting purposes and two if they go to prayer meetings regularly.
> After 14 hours' work spare time should be devoted to reading good literature.

4 CONTRASTS EXPRESSED IN PROVERBS AND QUOTATIONS

 a   All the following proverbs, aphorisms and quotes express a contrast. Can you express their meaning in your own words? (Some sayings also occur in other units.)

   i   The grass is always greener on the other side of the fence.
   ii Experience is not what happens to a man. It is what a man does with what happens to him. (*Aldous Huxley*)
   iii The best man for a man and the best man for a woman are not the same. (*José Ortega y Gasset*)
   iv No one has ever loved anyone the way everyone wants to be loved. (*Mignon McLaughlin*)
   v   We promise according to our hopes, and perform according to our fears. (*Duc François de La Rochefoucauld*)
   vi Military intelligence is a contradiction in terms.
   vii You start by sinking into his arms and end up with your arms in his sink.

 b   Discuss the contrasts expressed in these cartoons:

C LISTENING ACTIVITIES

1. There are many different ways of approaching problems and attempting to find solutions. One innovative way of thinking is that expounded by Dr Edward de Bono – *lateral* thinking. Dr de Bono now runs the largest curriculum programme in the world for the direct teaching of thinking in schools. His works have been translated into 19 languages.

    The lecture you are about to hear poses two problems. You will be asked to provide your own solution.

2. Listen to the lecture again. This time, make notes of the lecturer's comments as to similarities and differences between lateral and vertical thinking. Here is an example of one way to approach the problem:

    Lateral   *Vertical*
    Creative   Selective

3. Discuss your conclusions with your fellow students. Then give your own examples from your experience.

D STRUCTURE AND LANGUAGE USAGE

1 THE LANGUAGE OF CONTRAST (see Study Notes, page 37)

Make new sentences with more or less the same meaning but including the words given below each:

a Everybody's advised against doing it but I'm still going ahead.
   i nevertheless   ii even though

b Fifty years ago people used to make their own entertainment but nowadays they sit passively in front of their television.
   i whereas   ii unlike

c Although they promised to have it finished by the end of this week it now looks extremely unlikely.
   i despite   ii in spite

d I agree that it isn't ideal but it's the best in the circumstances.
   i even though   ii might

e Perhaps he is very gifted but he needn't be so rude.
   i even if   ii may

f They differ in musical tastes: whereas he likes jazz and country and western, his wife prefers soul and reggae.
   i unlike   ii on the other hand

EVEN THOUGH, EVEN IF . . .

g   The new manager's approach to problems is very different from his predecessor's.
    i   differ   ii   contrast (verb)
h   I can't tell the difference between soul and reggae.
    i   differentiate   ii   distinguish
i   Members of the club should be treated in exactly the same way. (There ....)
    i   distinction   ii   difference(s)
j   (Talking about a student's essay) I'm not sure you've always kept 'explanation' distinct from 'process'.
    i   discriminate   ii   distinction

2   BUT . . .

a   A second part of these sentences, which contrasts in some way with the first part, can be used to complete them. Make suggestions as for completing them.

Example: Ideally, we'd like to invest in that kind of activity, but we just haven't got the financial resources/but the present economic climate is hardly conducive to it.

  i   Theoretically, it's perfectly feasible ....
  ii   Superficially, you couldn't meet a nicer person ....
  iii Outwardly, he was totally calm and in control ....
  iv   Officially, he's at a conference in the City of London ....
  v   Technically, he's a very good player ....

b   In conversation we often try to anticipate objections by saying, for example, 'I don't want to pry, but how much do you earn?' The first part of the sentence (saying the speaker doesn't want to pry) contrasts strongly with the second (prying).

Discuss different ways of completing the following disarmers.

Example: I don't want to bother you, but can you help with my car?

  i   I know it's none of my business, but ....
  ii   I don't want to hurt your feelings, but ....
  iii   Of course I'm grateful for what you've done, but ....
  iv   At the risk of seeming inquisitive, ...
  v   Far be it from me to interfere in your personal affairs, but ....
  vi   I don't want to appear greedy, but ....
  vii   It's not up to me to criticise, but ....
  viii You know I'm not nosy, but ....

E WRITING ACTIVITIES

1 Refer to Reading Text A. Write a short composition (minimum 300 words) on class in your own country, using as many as possible of the new terms you have learned.

2 EXTENSION: TEXT IMPROVEMENT

The following text, about the 1986 World Motor Racing Championship, is rather repetitious (for example in its over-use of 'but'); it also tends to under-use other expressions of contrast. Write out the text again *varying* the expressions of contrast by using one of the alternatives given and making any necessary changes.

THE ADELAIDE GRAND PRIX NOVEMBER 1986

(a) At all the other Grand Prix this season the weather had been perfect but in Adelaide there was the constant threat of rain. Mansell had his problems at the (b) starts of the other races but everything went perfectly for him in preparation for (c) Adelaide.

(d) In Mexico his Honda engine had been tuned to deliver 1,100 horsepower but (e) in Adelaide it was set to produce appreciably less (f) but Mansell was faster, (g) recording the best average speed in practice and achieving the starting position he wanted. Mansell's two rivals for the World Championship both had to win to have (h) a chance (i) but Mansell only had to come third to clinch it. With only 10 minutes to go and in third place, Mansell was sitting pretty but fate then dealt the favourite a (j) cruel blow when his tyre blew up at 200 mph. He didn't slam on the brakes and hold the wheel rigid as you or I would have done but zig-zagged to a controlled stop, lucky to be alive.

a Unlike all (placed at beginning of text)
   Here . . ./(start new sentence)
b Whereas . . ./
   Mansell may . . . but everything/
   Mansell might . . . but everything . . .
c this race/
   his championship bid
d but over here in . . ./
   but for this Grand Prix
e although/
   even though/
   despite the fact that . . .
f nevertheless/
   still
g by far the best . . ./
   far and away the best
h in contrast to Mansell/
   Mansell, by contrast,/
   on the other hand/
   while
i Apparently/
   It seemed that . . ./
   To all appearances,
j Instead of/
   Whereas you or I might . . .

2 STUDY NOTES

3 EXTENSION: COMPARISON (see Study Notes, page 37)

Write a brief comparison (approximately 100 words) of one of the following pairs, taking care to use as many different ways of expressing contrast as possible.

The imaginative and the unimaginative mind
The analytical and the subjective mind
The good and bad businessman
The skilled and unskilled negotiator

STUDY NOTES

B1 CLASS CONSCIOUSNESS

Useful vocabulary for discussion

a less rigid social divisions; society is freer; to have the 'right' background; people from a 'good' family; the way you speak; to speak with a certain accent; if your family's got money; to come from a wealthy background

c to display your wealth; to achieve status on merit; to look down on people; consider them your social inferiors; to move up the social ladder; to make it (colloquial); to defer to your 'betters' (colloquial); to behave deferentially towards; to begrudge somebody something

d to change your car; exotic holiday destinations; send your children to expensive schools

e I regard/see them as; To me they're . . .; an evil; an anachronism in the modern world; faceless and characterless

f a pipe-dream

g to belong to a class

B2 CONTRASTS IN INTELLIGENCE

Useful vocabulary for discussion

c an analytical/well-disciplined mind; highly imaginative; extraordinary intellectual or creative power(s); ingenious; problem-solving skills; active intelligence; imaginative understanding; able to think on his/her feet (colloquial); sympathetic understanding; knowledgeable; to have good judgement in human affairs; spiritual perception; to have a good head for figures; great intuition/intuitive powers; an inventive mind; a visualising ability

B3 PAST AND PRESENT

Useful vocabulary for discussion

a literacy; numeracy; the skills for the job; literary education; a cultured mind; literary and linguistic skills; the ability to express yourself in good style; emphasis on the written word; ability to spell and to write legibly; information technology; computerised offices; computer terminals

D1 THE LANGUAGE OF CONTRAST

Study the following sentences and then use the information they provide on structures when completing D1.

All the evidence was against it; *nevertheless* we decided to give it a try; all the evidence was against it, but we *nevertheless* decided to give it a try; we decided to give it a try *nevertheless*. *Even though* it had been done many times before, we still wanted to do it for our own satisfaction. *Whereas* Americans will drive 150 km for an evening's entertainment, most English people think 50 km is too far. *Unlike* her sisters, Margaret has got considerable musical talent. *Unlike* London, where you can dine and dance until dawn, Edinburgh is relatively quiet after midnight. *In spite of/despite* having almost no money, they managed to have a very good time. *You might/may* not approve of it, but you'll still have to implement it when the time comes. *Even if* you get rid of class attitudes based on family background, there will still be social divisions based on money. Mark likes active holidays: his wife, *on the other hand*, prefers lazing beside a swimming pool.

The General Manager and the Financial Manager *differ* markedly in their attitudes to pay and conditions. The recent performance of the parent company *contrasts* dramatically with that of its subsidiaries. How do you *differentiate/distinguish* between the male and female of the species? There's a slight *difference* in coloration. All the racegoers should be able to make use of all the bars and restaurants on the course without *distinction*. There should be no *distinction* made between applicants on grounds of social class.

E3 EXTENSION: COMPARISON

His father and brothers have got good analytical minds; Jim, *by contrast*, is much woollier (colloquial) but much more fun with it. We've had some sizzling (colloquial) weather this summer, *in contrast* to last year. Let's sort it out now *rather than* in a couple of days' time. He's got a good brain as *opposed to/as distinct from* creative imagination. Actually it's been quite a good year for business, *contrary to* predictions.

3 LOGICAL RELATIONS

Discussing influences, reasons, causes, results, assumptions and scenarios, how we convey meanings non-verbally

A READING TEXTS

1 READING

See Unit 1, Section A (page 5) for instructions. Text B for this unit will be found on page 171.

Text A

REAPING A WHIRLWIND

The wave of violent behaviour in the wake of football matches and other public gatherings, epitomised by the Brussels outrage, had causes which we must identify if we are to find remedies. One is an erosion of social disciplines which characterised the third quarter of this century. Historical parallels must be used with care. But in matters of public behaviour great improvement occurred between the middle of the last century and the middle of this one. Mob violence and crime declined. Respectability became the watchword among the relatively new class of urban wage-earners, due partly to the spread of evangelical Christianity, the strong family, growing prosperity, improved schooling, pride in Queen and Empire and the institution of an unarmed civil police.

   The post-1945 settlement embodied a reversal of these trends. It became fashionable among the middle classes to sneer at family, respectability and middle-class values, pre-marital chastity, social disciplines, neatness and thrift. 'Middle class' became a term of abuse; permissiveness, indiscipline, an anti-police mood, were imparted from the top downwards. They should not have been surprised when what the Victorian middle classes called the 'lower orders', but to whom they had a sense of responsibility, took those who set intellectual and political fashions in this country at their word. For a couple of decades our political classes have refused to accept the evidence of their own eyes. They have blamed these phenomena on 'deprivation', discrimination, unemployment, bad housing, the police – on anything except the erosion of social disciplines brought about by their own mood of rebellion against established values.

They failed to understand that ordinary people need simple rules to live by, and that without a framework of social discipline they very easily become brutalised. In many societies, discipline is imposed from outside by large, repressive police forces, heavy sentences, social penalties of all kinds. The public here are now calling for draconian measures. The Government will have to ask itself whether it can any longer afford to permit the mass gatherings which now seem to generate a mob psychology. But above all we must turn our minds towards regenerating the largely self-enforcing social and moral disciplines built up by previous generations, without which reliance on repressive disciplines will almost certainly gain credence as a lesser evil.

Leader from *The Daily Telegraph*, 3 June 1985

2 QUESTIONS ON THE TEXTS

TEXT A

a 'Historical parallels must be used with care', the writer says. But does he use them with care?

b One person after reading the article said: "What patronising rubbish! Thinks we're a lot of kids who need daddy's rules or we get into trouble!' What do you think of her response?

c Where would you say the writer stands politically: far left, left, left of centre, right of centre, far right? Give reasons for your opinion.

TEXT B

Give in very general terms an account of the various theories about the origin of human life, basing your account on the facts given in Text B.

B COMMUNICATIVE ACTIVITIES

1 INFLUENCES (see Study Notes, page 55)

a Which of the following were particularly formative regarding the ideas which now guide your life?

  i   mother
  ii father
  iii school/university
  iv a religious institution
  v   contemporaries

ADDUCING CAUSES

b Which ideas were you inculcated with about the following:

   i   the family
   ii the importance of education
   iii choice of career
   iv money
   v clothes
   vi food and drink
   vii male and female roles

c How strong are the influences you talked about in (b) above in your life *now*? Are there any more recent influences in your life that have made you change your ideas?

d How do/did/would you try to influence your children? In particular, how would that influence differ from the way you were influenced as a child?

'Some people would blame your genes, others your home environment, but I blame you, Wimpole, plain and simple.'

2 CAUSAL LINKS (see Study Notes, page 55)

A

Say what connections are typically made between the two parts of the following, and then discuss whether you agree with those links.

Example: Drug abuse/crime

Drug abuse often leads to *crime* because the drug-user needs money to pay for his or her addiction.

   i   social deprivation/high crime rates
   ii a happy childhood/a happy adulthood
   iii junk food/disturbed behaviour in children
   iv sightings of UFOs (unidentified flying objects)/life in another part of the universe
   v violence on TV, video, and in films/increasing number of crimes of violence
   vi the increasing wealth of the West/poverty and starvation in developing countries

B INTERRELATIONS

Say how each item in the following diagrams usually interacts with every other. For example, when *inflation goes up, money incomes* and *retail prices* usually go up too, but *real income* might well go down. (There may be no interaction; when, in your opinion, this is the case say so and justify your opinion.)

i

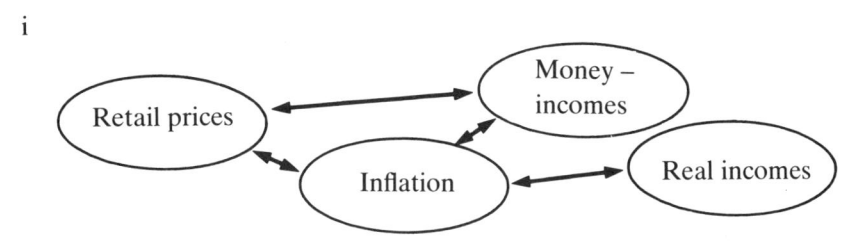

- Retail prices ↔ Money-incomes
- Retail prices ↔ Inflation
- Inflation ↔ Money-incomes
- Inflation ↔ Real incomes

ii

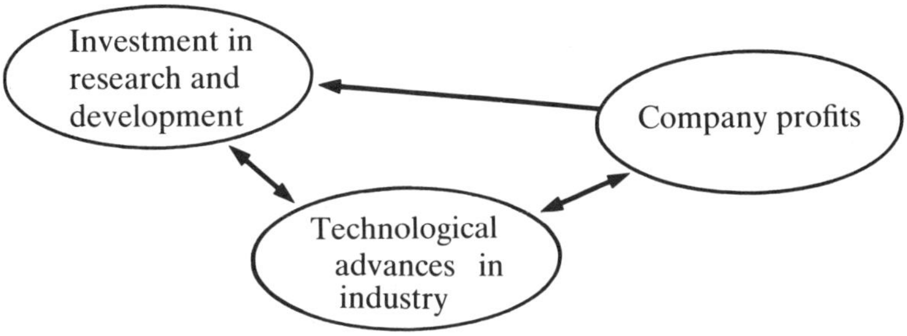

- Company profits → Investment in research and development
- Investment in research and development ↔ Technological advances in industry
- Company profits ↔ Technological advances in industry

iii

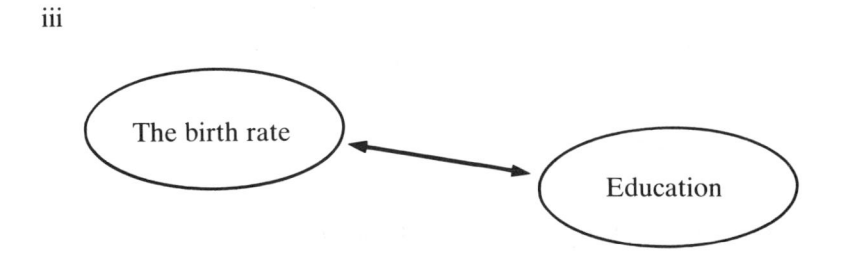

- The birth rate ↔ Education

iv

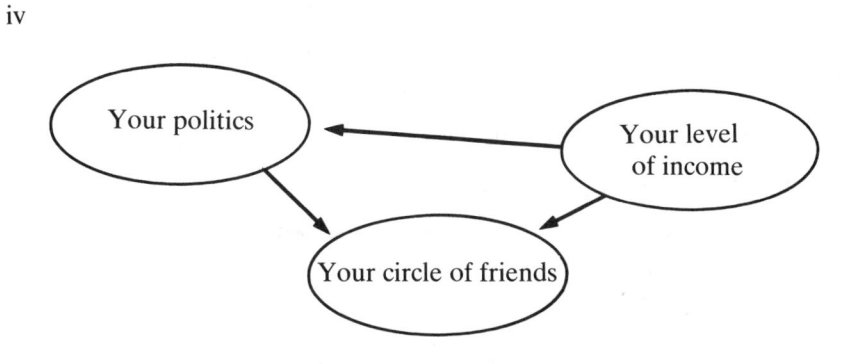

- Your politics ↔ Your level of income
- Your politics → Your circle of friends
- Your level of income → Your circle of friends

TALKING ABOUT CAUSE AND EFFECT   CONDITIONALS

C WRITING SCENARIOS

The word *scenario* used in this way means a situation that might develop logically from a series of events. The typical scenario-writer tries to show how a certain situation might evolve step by step from the present state of affairs. This technique is particularly useful for studying possible military, political and sociological developments, where it provides an important input to forward planning. For example, a sociologist specialising in welfare provision might foresee the following possible 'steps', each of which partly or wholly results from the other:

i   A continued fall in the birth rate.

ii   An ageing population.

iii   Demand for more financial resources to support social security, health and community services for the elderly.

iv   Substantial increases in taxes.

Discuss possible scenarios with the following subjects. Each scenario should consist of at least three steps.

i   developments in personal transport (cars etc.)

ii   developments in communication technology

iii   the next world war

iv   employment

v   medical developments including replacement surgery

D DOES IT FOLLOW?

Are the following assumptions tenable or untenable? Say exactly in which way they are true or untrue, in your opinion.

i   The nicest people are the most popular.

ii   The longer you do a job, the better you become at doing it.

iii   Absence makes the heart grow fonder. (Proverb)

iv   The cleverest people have had the longest education.

v   Interviewing panels select the best candidates for the job.

vi   People who are religious are more gentle and civilised than those who aren't.

vii   People grow wiser with age.

viii   Women are gentler than men.

ix   You must be in love with your partner when you get married.

3 REPRESENTING RELATIONS (see Study Notes, page 56)

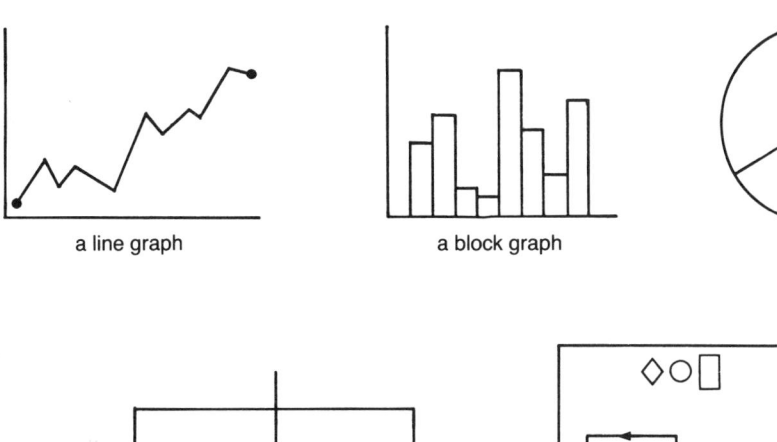

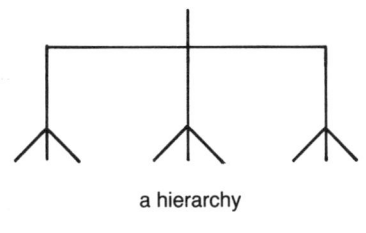

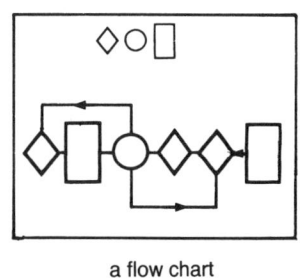

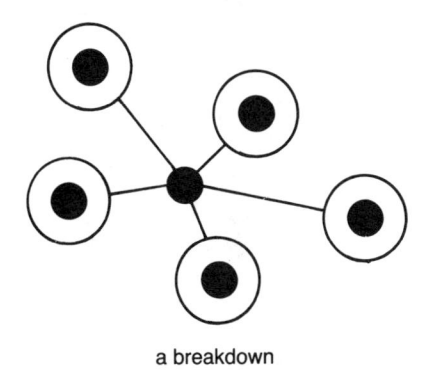

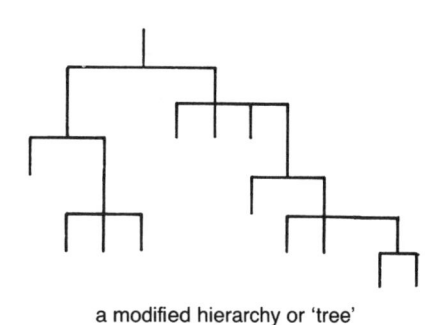

- a line graph
- a block graph
- a pie chart
- a hierarchy
- a flow chart
- a breakdown
- a modified hierarchy or 'tree'

a Discuss which of the above modes of representation would generally be suitable for:
  i   displaying the components of, for example, an organisation, without showing their relative importance.
  ii showing the relationship between only two variables.
  iii displaying a historical development.
  iv showing a chain of command.
  v   comparing the size of the various sections of a whole.
  vi indicating what happens at each stage.

DISCUSSING GRAPHS etc.

b If we wanted to display the following information visually, which of the modes of representation would be particularly suitable?

i The processing of job applications received by a company.
ii A comparison of the number of video recorders per 100 inhabitants, in the EEC member states.
iii The line of command in a central police station.
iv Annual rainfall on a month-by-month basis.
v The distribution of several staff categories (e.g. production workers, clerical, administrative) within a company, emphasising relative numerical importance.
vi The administrative structure of a large company.
vii The activities of one multinational company, stressing their variety rather than their importance.

c Relate the various modes of representation to the different aspects of the activities of the following:
i a university
ii a company

Example: Army: *A line graph* could be used to show the changes in its size over the last 50 years. A *block graph* might be used to compare expenditure on the army in the leading industrial nations; a *pie chart* would show what proportion of total expenditure on the army was spent on salaries, equipment, transport, medical services etc.

4 READING THE SIGNS (see Study Notes, page 56)

A SUMMING UP

We all become experts at summing up situations very quickly: whenever we walk into a room full of unfamiliar people we make instant judgements about, for example, who is in charge or who will give us the assistance we need.

Discuss the answers to the questions below and explain how you reached your conclusion.

i Are they together or not?

DISCUSSING GRAPHS, CHARTS etc.

ii   Who are the two most senior people in the office?

iii   Who is the teacher?

NON-VERBAL MESSAGES

B LETTING PEOPLE KNOW (see Study Notes, page 56)

1. What are the various non-verbal ways (body language, eye movements and expressions) we use to show:
    i   a new person we meet socially in a group of other people that we particularly like them.
    ii   that we are emotionally very close to the person we are with and perhaps would prefer to be alone with him or her.
    iii   without being too obviously rude, that we do not wish to talk to somebody who is insisting on talking to us.
    iv   that we are sympathetic to, for example, somebody's problems.
    v   that we are listening carefully to what a boss, lecturer etc. is saying (even if we aren't).

2. What do the following mean when we see or hear them?
    i sighs   ii yawns   iii glares   iv nods   v winks
    vi frowns   vii blushes   viii stares

C WHAT'S HAPPENED?

Say what you think has just happened to cause the following expressions:

i

ii

iii iv

3

47

5 OLD-FASHIONED LOGIC

The following poem, 'Common Sense', was written, or as the poet says 'compiled', by Alan Brownjohn (a contemporary poet) after browsing through an old arithmetic manual. Read it and discuss what it has to say about the England of 70 years ago.

Common Sense

An agricultural labourer, who has
A wife and four children, receives 20s a week.
¾ buys food, and the members of the family
Have three meals a day.
How much is that person per meal?
               – FROM PITMAN'S COMMON SENSE ARITHMETIC 1917

A gardener, paid 24s a week, is
Fined 1/3 if he comes to work late.
At the end of 26 weeks, he receives
£30.5.3. How
Often was he late?
               – FROM PITMAN'S COMMON SENSE ARITHMETIC 1917

A milk dealer buys milk at 3d a quart. He
Dilutes it with 3% water and sells
4 gallons of the mixture at
4d per quart. How much of his profit is made by
Adulterating the milk?
               – FROM PITMAN'S COMMON SENSE ARITHMETIC 1917

The table printed below gives the number
Of paupers in the United Kingdom, and
The total cost of poor relief.
Find the average number
Of paupers per ten thousand people.
               – FROM PITMAN'S COMMON SENSE ARITHMETIC 1917

3

Out of an army of 28,000 men,
15% were
Killed, 25% were
Wounded. Calculate
How many men there were left to fight.
　　　　　– FROM PITMAN'S COMMON SENSE ARITHMETIC 1917

These sums are offered to
That host of young people in our Elementary Schools, who
Are so ardently desirous of setting
Foot upon the first rung of the
Educational ladder. . .
　　　　　– FROM PITMAN'S COMMON SENSE ARITHMETIC 1917

An army had to march to the relief of
A besieged town, 500 miles away, which
Had telegraphed that it could hold out for 18 days.
The army made forced marches at the rate of 18
Miles a day. Would it be there in time?
　　　　　– FROM PITMAN'S COMMON SENSE ARITHMETIC 1917

'Common Sense', *Collected Poems 1952–83*, Alan Brownjohn, Secker & Warburg,

6 ARGUMENTATION BY IMAGES

The following photographs, published in different magazines, seek to provoke certain thoughts or discussions. What are those thoughts or discussions?

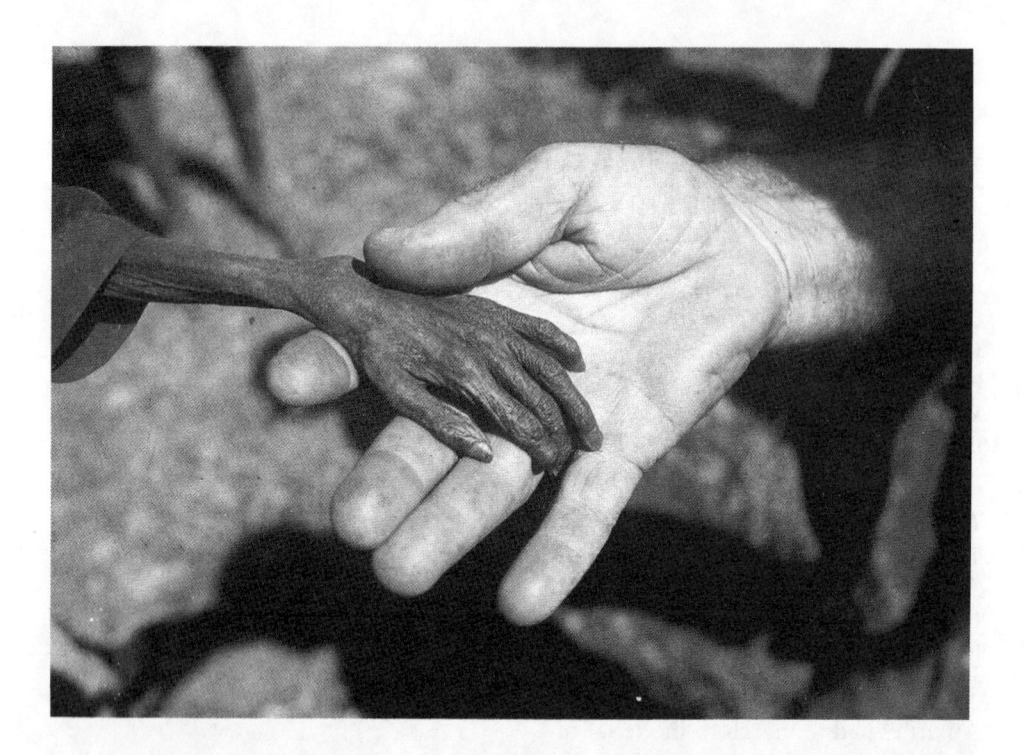

C LISTENING ACTIVITIES

Humour often depends on what may *seem* to be logical deduction, but with a sting in the tail. That 'sting' is represented by the personal and idiosyncratic ways we have of making deductions. Communication tends to break down when we fail to understand another person's point of view or cannot share common terms of reference.

These activities should help you to experience different ways of making deductions.

1   Listen to a story which may or may not be true. Then work in pairs or groups of three to attempt to reach agreement on the following questions:

a   Why do you think the man asked a policeman for advice?
b   How logical does the policeman's interpretation of the question seem to you?
c   What were the differences in terms of reference between the man and the policeman?
d   What words lead to the difference in interpretation?
e   What other interpretations could be made?

2 a   Now listen and do exactly as you are told. When you have finished, there will be certain activities to be attempted.

   b   Listen very carefully to a second set of instructions. At the end, you will be asked to justify any answers.

D STRUCTURE AND LANGUAGE USAGE

THE LANGUAGE OF CAUSE, REASON, EFFECT AND PURPOSE

1   Make new sentences with approximately the same meaning to include the words given below each example.

   a   Sorry, I didn't mean to do that!
      i   intend   ii   deliberately   iii   intentional

   b   This will necessitate cutting down on expenditure all round.
      i   necessary   ii   mean (verb)   iii   involve

   c   To this day the police still have no idea why the crime was committed.
      i   explanation   ii   motive

   d   We're trying for a £3 million turnover this year.
      i   target (noun)   ii   achieve   iii   aim (verb)

   e   How will these changes affect our company?
      i   effect (noun)   ii   consequences

VERB PATTERNS – INTEND, MEAN, INVOLVE, AIM

f Why are we having all these meetings?
   i purpose   ii reason (noun)
g These attitudes seem to colour a lot of her thoughts and actions.
   i shape (verb)   ii lie behind

2 Match one of the items below with each of the sentences and use it to paraphrase the sentence, making any necessary changes.

   motivation   conclusion(s)   incentive   ulterior motive   goal

a What's the point in doing it? – You don't *get anything in return*.
b I don't want to seem cynical, but what does he *really want*?
c His students seem to lack any *interest in their work*.
d I don't quite understand *his reasoning*.
e I've achieved *everything in life I wanted to*.

3 IF . . .

Suggest possible Conditional 3 sentences prompted by the following. There is often more than one possibility.

a Jim's wife thinks that his missing the train and being 45 minutes late for the interview was the reason why he was turned down for the job. Jim's wife thinks that if Jim ....
b Jim, however, thinks he was too argumentative during the interview.
c The actual reason he wasn't offered the job was that he lacked experience with the latest technology, especially in the area of robotics.
d Some historians maintain that President Kennedy's assassination saved him from the unpopularity that would have come to him as a result of US involvement in Vietnam.
e The *Titanic*'s distress-signals were not picked up by more ships in the area because seventy years ago ships' radios were not manned 24 hours a day.
f The 1986 *Challenger* space-shuttle disaster was caused by unusually low temperatures immediately before the launch.
g The rubber seals on the booster rockets were damaged, causing a fuel leak.
h At school he was given very little encouragement to follow the career of his choice, resulting in his wasting several years in the wrong job.
i A man accused of taking part in a supermarket robbery decided to save money by dispensing with a lawyer and defending himself. While cross-examining the supermarket manager, however, he lost his temper and shouted at him: 'I should have blown your head right off . . .', adding after a moment 'If I'd been there . . .' But this afterthought didn't impress the jury, who found him guilty. (True story, USA, 1986)

4   Make new sentences of approximately the same meaning as the first, using the vocabulary given.

a   The traditional social disciplines have been eroded leading to a general rebellion against established values.
   i   ……… resulting ………
   ii   ……… as a consequence ………
   iii The erosion ………
   iv   The traditional social disciplines having ………

b   We must regenerate the largely self-enforcing social and moral disciplines or the argument for repression will gain acceptance.
   i   If we fail ………
   ii   Unless ………
   iii ……… to prevent ………
   iv   ……… in case ………

c   In our opinion the standards of state education have fallen in recent years, so we're saving up to give our children a private education.
   i   Seeing that ………
   ii   Standards ……… having ……… years ………
   iii The reason we're saving up ………

E WRITING ACTIVITIES

1 (Reading Text A)

a   Write a summary of the article 'Reaping the Whirlwind' in approximately 120–150 words.

b   Complete the following sentences using the content (but not necessarily the exact words) of Reading Text A. Sometimes the same content is repeated in order to provide extra practice with the structures of the unit.
   i   If we are to find remedies for this violent behaviour we must ………
   ii   It is only by identifying the causes that ………
   iii   The spread of evangelical Christianity, the strong family, growing prosperity and improved schooling ……… in matters of public behaviour.
   iv   The post-1945 settlement led to ………
   v   Unless ordinary people ……… brutalised.
   vi   Since we do not in the UK impose discipline from outside ……… social and moral disciplines.
   vii   If we fail to regenerate these disciplines ………
   viii In order to prevent reliance on repressive disciplines gaining credence the largely ………

UNLESS/IN CASE/SEEING THAT …

2 EXTENSION: APHORISMS AND PROVERBS

Paraphrase the following aphorisms, proverbs etc. using a sentence containing the word 'if'.

a   Show me the child and I will show you the man.

b   Everyone has talent at 25. The difficulty is to have it at 50.

c   Laugh and the world laughs with you, cry and you cry alone.

d   To be a leader of men one must turn one's back on men.

e   No great man ever complains of want of opportunity.

f   There's no smoke without fire.

g   People who live in glass houses shouldn't throw stones.

3 EXTENSION. TEXT COMPLETION

a   The following text does not 'hang together' as it should because certain items have been omitted. Study it carefully and complete the text and rewrite it using *all* of the items in the box at least once.

bred	associated	necessitated	brought about	caused
led to	created	[in order] to	so [that]	conducive [to]

In the mid-eighteenth century the interaction of social, scientific and economic developments conditions that were to the occurrence of what we now call 'The Industrial Revolution': Labour resources had been by the changing patterns of agricultural production and ownership on the land that opportunities for work in the new Northern towns immediately an influx of job-seekers from both the country and Ireland. Recently invented textile machinery with such names as Arkwright that factories be built house them. But there was a price to pay for these developments: Insanitary conditions and overcrowding in these jerry-built towns disease; deprivation and social conflict.

b   Using the above completed text as a model, write a similar text of your own explaining how *one* of the following phenomena come or might come about:

   i   Earthquakes

   ii   Nuclear-generated electricity

   iii Famines in Africa

   iv   Permanent world peace

STUDY NOTES

B1 INFLUENCES

Useful language for discussion

a I was particularly influenced by . . .; My father had a strong influence on me . . .; I suppose my school gave me a lot of my ideas . . .

b   i   Looking after your family is the most important thing.
     iii   To make the right choice from the start; to go into the army; to become a lawyer; to choose an academic career; to follow in my father's footsteps.
     iv   Not to waste money; to use money well; to look after it; not to be mean; 'look after the pennies and the pounds will look after themselves' (Saying).
     v   Not to waste money on looking smart; that good clothes are always worth paying for; that it is your character that matters not your clothes.
     vi   Moderation; importance of being a good host/hostess.
     vii   The woman's place is in the home; it's the man's job to provide for his wife and family; the wife shouldn't have to go out to work.

d to instil ideas/principles in people; to give children the same kind of upbringing; to give them a 'framework'; to emphasise different values; to allow them more independence

B2 CAUSAL LINKS

Useful language for discussion

a cause; lead to; create; conducive to; is likely to lead to; is said to lead to; has been established as a cause; is taken as evidence for; is held responsible for; some people see it as causing . . .; affect

b Interrelations

Notes on vocabulary

Real income is income in terms of what you can buy with it so that if the cost of living goes down and your money income remains the same your real income rises. Research and Development is often abbreviated to R and D.

'Education' in (iii) may be interpreted as 'The need for educational places' or as 'average educational levels'.

Useful vocabulary for discussion

increase; go up; rise; fall; go down; remain steady; might be associated with; have the effect of + *ing*; educational provision; to move in different social circles; to move up the social ladder

c Writing scenarios

When you come to write your scenarios, remember that each step *should partly or wholly result from the last step.*

Useful vocabulary

    i   exhaust oil resources; oil begins to run out; traffic congestion becomes impossible; one-man helicopters
    ii   pocket-sized; videophones; word-processors; computer networks; call up; get into contact with . . .; to work from home
    iii a proliferation of nuclear weapons; a local 'flare-up'; superpowers; 'client regimes'; the conflict escalates; to be drawn into a conflict
    iv part-time work; job-sharing; working from home; self-employment; the service industries
    v   'spare-part' or replacement surgery; life expectancy; routine operations; overpopulation

d Does it follow?

Useful vocabulary for discussion

It doesn't necessarily follow; it isn't necessarily true; it doesn't always work quite like that; on the contrary, . . .; the opposite might be more true; it depends . . .

B3 REPRESENTING RELATIONS

Useful vocabulary for discussion

  c   i   student numbers; staff numbers; accommodation; faculties; administrative structure; application procedures; degree courses, research, research degrees
        ii production; productivity; unit costs; profitability; diversified activities; production process; administrative structure; staff grades; group structure; associated companies

B4 READING THE SIGNS

Useful vocabulary for discussion

  a   the way he's/she's (sitting); the way their legs are pointing; their expressions; you can tell by . . .; it's obvious from . . .; the way everybody else is . . .; he must be the teacher . . .
  b   1   eye contact; attentive; give a lot of attention to; hold hands; stand close; talk in a low voice to; avoid eye contact; keep looking around; nod approvingly; put on a very serious expression; laugh at any jokes; look very thoughtful
       2   boredom; embarrassment; anger; assent; curiosity; disapproval; exasperation; perplexity; complicity

4 OMISSION

Talking about omissions, human failings; eradicating problems; deprivation

A READING TEXTS

1 READING

See Unit 1, Section A (page 5) for instructions. Text B for this unit will be found on page 172.

Text A

THE ACADEMIC by William Hazlitt

His ears are nailed to his books; and deadened with the sound of the Greek and Latin tongues, and the din and smithery of school-learning. Does he know anything more of poetry? He knows the number of feet in a verse, and of acts in a play; but of the soul or spirit he knows nothing. He can turn a Greek ode into English, or a Latin epigram into Greek verse; but whether either is worth the trouble he leaves to the critics. Does he understand 'the act and practique part of life' better than 'the theorique'? No. He knows no liberal or mechanic art, no trade or occupation, no game of skill or chance. Learning has no skill, in agriculture, in building, in working in wood or in iron; it cannot make any instrument of labour, or use it when made; it cannot handle the plough or the spade, or the chisel or the hammer; it knows nothing of hunting or hawking, fishing or shooting, of horses or dogs, of fencing or dancing, or cudgel-playing, or bowls, or cards, or tennis, or anything else. The learned professor of all arts and sciences cannot reduce any one of them to practice, though he may contribute an account of them to an Encyclopaedia. He has not the use of his hands nor of his feet; he can neither run, nor walk, nor swim; and he considers all those who actually understand and can exercise any of these arts of body or mind as vulgar and mechanical men – though to know almost any one of them in perfection requires long time and practice, and a turn of mind particularly devoted to them. It does not require more than this to enable the learned candidate to arrive, by painful study, at a doctor's degree and a fellowship, and to eat, drink, and sleep the rest of his life!

The thing is plain. All that men really understand is confined to a very small compass; to their daily affairs and experiences; to what they have an opportunity to know, and motives to study or practise. The rest is affectation and imposture. The common people have the use of their limbs; for they live by their labour or skill. They understand their own business and the characters of those they have to deal with; for it is necessary that they should. They have eloquence to express their passions, and wit at will to express their contempt and provoke laughter. Their natural use of speech is not hung up in monumental mockery, in an obsolete language; nor is their sense of what is ludicrous, or readiness at finding out allusions to express it. You will hear more good things on the outside of a stage-coach from London to Oxford than if you were to pass a twelvemonth with the undergraduates, or heads of colleges, of that famous university; and more home truths are to be learnt from listening to a noisy debate in an alehouse than from attending to a formal one in the House of Commons. An elderly gentlewoman will often know more of character, and be able to illustrate it by more amusing anecdotes taken from the history of what has been said, done, and gossiped in a country town for the last fifty years, than the best blue-stocking of the age will be able to glean from that sort of learning which consists in an acquaintance with all the novels and satirical poems published in the same period.

To conclude this subject. The most sensible people to be met with in society are men of business and of the world, who argue from what they see and know, instead of spinning cobweb distinctions of what things ought to be. Women have often more of what is called good sense than men. They have fewer pretensions; are less implicated in theories; and judge of objects more from their immediate and involuntary impression on the mind, and, therefore, more truly and naturally. They cannot reason wrong; for they do not reason at all. They do not think or speak by rule; and they have in general more eloquence and wit, as well as sense, on that account.

William Hazlitt, *Table Talk*

2 QUESTIONS ON THE TEXTS

TEXT A

a   Hazlitt says 'You will hear more good things on the outside of a stage-coach from London to Oxford than if you were to pass a twelvemonth [= year] with the undergraduates, or heads of colleges of that famous university. In what sense does Hazlitt mean this? Is Hazlitt being fair?

b   Judging from the style of English, how long ago would you say this text was written? Which of the following is approximately right – 300 years ago, 200 years ago, 100 years ago, 70 years ago?

TEXT B

a   Is the overall mood of the story optimistic, pessimistic or neutral in your opinion?

b   Would you say this is a story with a message or a story told to entertain?

c   Can you see any evidence in present trends in lifestyles in the USA, Western Europe or Japan for the way of life described by Bradbury?

BOTH TEXTS

a 'Hazlitt and Bradbury are both social critics and moralists.' How far do you agree?

b Imagine visitors from Hazlitt's time and Bradbury's 2053 could visit each other's periods. What do you think each would particularly miss, not only in physical but also in human terms?

B COMMUNICATIVE ACTIVITIES

1 IMPROVING CONDITIONS (see Study Notes, page 71)

The Earl of Shaftesbury (1801–85) reformer and philanthropist

Mother Theresa (born 1911) has devoted her life to helping the poor of Calcutta

William Wilberforce MP (1759–1833) campaigned for abolition of the slave trade (1807) and the emancipation of existing slaves (1833)

In every age there are idealistic individuals and groups who seek to improve society by eradicating what they see as 'problems'. 100–150 years ago in Britain people such as the Earl of Shaftesbury campaigned to abolish harsh working practices. Among these were the employment of six-year-old children as coal miners or chimney sweeps, or making young women work in the mines for 14 hours a day. Later in life he worked to provide some basic education for the children of the poor.

Other problems of that age were:

Slum housing – overcrowded and without basic amenities, causing diseases like cholera and typhoid.

Alcoholism – drink was cheap and offered an escape from intolerable social conditions.

Illiteracy – one estimate was that 60% of people getting married could not sign their own name.

Harsh working conditions – a 70-hour week 52 weeks of the year was not exceptional.

a   Consider the situation 100–150 years ago in either the country you live in or one you know well; what were the problems (social? medical? environmental?) that concerned people then and how did reformers set about eradicating them?

b   And now? There is considerable concern in the UK about, for example, unemployment, homelessness, drug abuse and racism, as well as diseases due to the modern lifestyle. What are the problems that particularly concern people in the country you live in at the present time and what is being done to eradicate them?

c   Can you relate the following to the topic under discussion?
  i   campaigns
  ii   pressure groups
  iii 'busybodies and do-gooders'

d   What motivates reformers? Do they try to help people out of altruism and unselfishness, or is it more complicated than that?

e   If we eliminated all the major problems – if all disease, famine, unemployment etc. were eradicated – would we all be happy? Give reasons for your answers.

2 WHAT'S THE PROBLEM? WHAT'S MISSING? (see Study Notes, page 71)

a   All the following suggest that something, often a quality of some kind, is lacking. Make suggestions as to what the problem is for each example and what might be done to remedy it if possible. Look at the two examples.

Example As usual, Samantha's typing was full of every conceivable kind of mistake.
= Her work *lacks care.*/She's got *poor concentration.*/She doesn't pay *enough attention to detail.*/She should take more care.

Example: Everybody else was absolutely helpless with laughter, but Simon sat there with a straight face, looking very disapproving.
He hasn't got much sense of humour./*He takes himself very seriously.*/*He's got no sense of fun.*/*He should stop taking himself so seriously.*

  i   Angela wanted to tell him just what she thought of his behaviour, but thought it might have consequences for her job.
  ii   Mark didn't discuss the difficult situation at work with his wife. Nor did he tell her about his decision to change his job until after he'd actually given notice.
  iii My uncle was the sort of man who put his wife's tears or moods either down to something she'd eaten or to the fact that she hadn't had enough fresh air recently.

iv   The insurance company you work for has finalised plans to move its head office from Central London to Manchester. There have been rumours, but none of the employees have been told officially. You now read the announcement in a newspaper.

v   When the couple upstairs come home at 2 or 3 a.m., they talk loudly and bang doors, waking up everybody in the house.

vi   A convicted murderer boasts of the crimes he has committed.

vii Our Chairman has the unhappy knack of creating a situation where half of the Committee are at the throats of the other half only about 20 minutes into the discussion.

viii After being in business for only a year, they found that their product was not the right one for the market and that, consequently, their new company was in jeopardy.

b   All the following are examples of behaviour which most people dislike being subjected to and which in some way or other involve absence.

i   being hung up on (colloquial)
ii   being snubbed
iii   being passed over
iv   being taken for granted
v   being patronised
vi   being manipulated
vii   being let down
viii being stood up (colloquial)
ix   being talked down to
x   being kept in the dark

i   Check the meanings and suggest possible contexts and examples for each.
ii   Where possible say how they involve the absence of something and what it is they are lacking.
iii   Have you had experience of any of the above? Tell the rest of the group. Which of those you have experienced do you particularly dislike?
iv   Can you add any more to the list? What?

c   How do you deal with the following circumstances?

i   Being totally on your own for long periods of time.
ii   The person you are talking to won't let his or her eyes meet yours.
iii   You are in a group that has to stay together, but awkward gaps keep appearing in the conversation when everybody looks round desperately trying to think of something to say.
iv   The person you're talking to asks you a lot of questions but doesn't bother to listen to the answers.
v   The person you're talking to finishes your sentences for you.

PASSIVE GERUND

3 IF ONLY...

The following article was written by a top British pop-star for a teenage magazine. Paul Young describes how at school his teachers actively discouraged him from taking up the career he wanted to and in which he has now been unusually successful.

Things I Wish I'd Known At
PAUL YOUNG 15

'I always regarded myself as being a good student when I was at school. I mean, I wasn't the kind of guy who messed around too much in class and I didn't play truant or anything like that. I realised that it was worthwhile buckling down and doing the work because the qualifications would at least come in handy if I couldn't do what I really wanted to do – sing!

'Also, keeping in the teachers' good books made life that bit easier! Which is why I thought that they'd be on my side when I told them of my hopes and plans, and do as much as possible to help me.

'I can remember quite clearly when we were asked to go and have a chat individually with the careers master. It was the usual chat about what we wanted to do and how to best get interviews or whatever. Well, I sat there quite innocently and told him that I wanted to be a singer. I didn't think there was anything all that unusual in this.

'But instead of being in any way enthusiastic, he just gave me a smile. Even then I thought he would surely offer some advice. However, he started laughing and told me things like that were fine for a hobby, but choosing singing for a career was quite ridiculous.

'That annoyed me tremendously, because I was really serious about it. Maybe it was the idea of being a pop singer that made him react that way. If I'd said that I wanted to be in Grand Opera he might have reacted differently!

'He launched into a long lecture about how singing was not a career. That I couldn't just leave school and become one. That the profession was full of uncertainty with absolutely no guarantee of success and that I'd be lucky to find any work at all!

'He kept on about how I had qualifications and that I ought to try for something sensible that would set me up for the rest of my life. I've never felt so despondent, especially when my own teacher backed him up.

'Eventually I was persuaded to go and do an engineering apprenticeship. The people there were friendly, but for years I was bored and frustrated and spent every spare hour involved with music.

'I just wish I'd known then that I didn't have to do something I didn't want to do. I can appreciate that singing is a dodgy career, but so is anything, these days – you are totally reliant on your own ability and a lot of luck! But that careers master could have been more helpful. Maybe suggested that I go to college to study drama and singing . . . or take a job and do singing lessons as well. Or even tried to direct me to getting a job with a recording company or something like that!

'I suppose I could have done all that myself if I'd thought about it but at fifteen you respect what older people tell you. I just wish now I had gone out on my own!'

from *Jackie* 1 June 1985

a   Read the text carefully.
b   Would you, if you were a careers teacher, give a student active encouragement to try to succeed as a pop singer?
c   What would your reaction as a parent or careers teacher be to a boy or girl whose ambition was to be a novelist or a painter but who also wanted to support a family?
d   Do any of the following apply to you? Tell the rest of the group (using, for example: 'I wish I'd . . .', 'I think if I'd . . .', 'Sometimes I think if I'd . . .', 'I regret not . . .', 'I do wish I'd . . .')
  i   You regret not taking up a different career.
  ii   There are ambitions that you would dearly like to have achieved.
  iii You regret the 'conditioning' you received as a child and would like your childhood to have been influenced in a different way.
  iv   You have talents you have been dissuaded from developing.
  v   You feel that other people could have given you more encouragement to do what you really wanted to do.

4 MAKE IT SNAPPY!

a   The following items have all been taken from newspapers and magazines. Notice how they cut language down to the absolute minimum by omitting, for example, 'Do you', 'Have you got', 'Are you'.
  i   Discuss what the full versions would be.
  ii   Make suggestions as to what is being advertised.

i   *MOVING HOUSE?*

ii **GETTING MARRIED?**

iii *SORE THROAT?*

iv **Want to retire where the grass is greener?**

v   MOVING OFFICES?

vi M.O.T. DUE?

ELLIPSIS etc.

b   Discuss what the following are advertising and make suggestions as to how they could be reduced in length to produce a 'snappier' version.
   i   Are you tired of package holidays?
   ii Are you totally satisfied with your pension arrangements?
   iii Are you having difficulty balancing your budget?
   iv Are you worried about your tax?
   v   Do you feel like a break?

c   In the same way we often reduce utterances to the bare minimum; at home we might say 'Cup of coffee?', 'Like a cup of coffee?' or just 'Coffee?', instead of 'Would you like a cup of coffee?'
   Discuss how you could reduce the following in a similar way. In many cases there is more than one possibility.
   i   Did you go into town?
   ii   Would you like a cigarette?
   iii Did you sleep well?
   iv   Was there a lot of traffic?
   v   Have you got change for £10?
   vi   Would you like a chocolate?
   vii Have you got the time?
   viii Do have another piece of cake.
   ix   I hope you have a good trip.
   x   Aren't you ready yet?

5 PRIVATION

Read the following poem and then discuss the answers to the questions below.

Touch

When I get out
I'm going to ask someone
   to touch me
   very gently please
   and slowly,
   touch me
   I want
   to learn again
   how life feels.
I've not been touched
for seven years
   for seven years
   I've been untouched
   out of touch
   and I've learnt
   to know now
   the meaning
   untouchable.

ELLIPSIS etc.

Untouched – not quite
I can count the things
that have touched me
One: fists
At the beginning
>fierce mad fists
>beating beating
>till I remember
>screaming
>don't touch me
>please don't touch me.

Two: paws
The first four years of paws
>every day
>patting paws, searching
>– arms up, shoes off
>legs apart –
>prodding paws, systematic
>heaving, indifferent
>probing away
>all privacy.

I don't want fists and paws
I want
>to want to be touched
>again
>and to touch.
>I want to feel alive
>again
>I want to say
>when I get out

Here I am
please touch me.

'Touch' Hugh Lewin, in *Poets to the People*: South African Freedom Poems, Barry Feinberg (ed), Heinemann Educational Books.

a   Discuss what you think the circumstances are that are described in the poem. Whose are the fists and the paws?

b   How do you think you would feel in the same or similar circumstances?

c   We are being invited to feel sympathy for the writer; does he deserve it?

C LISTENING ACTIVITIES

In the mini-dialogues you will hear, there are repeated examples of conclusions drawn from insufficient evidence. Your task is to listen for the occasions when real evidence has been omitted and when the spoken communication seems to be breaking down. Another possible reason for communication breakdown is that we seldom share experiences and values.

1   In the following five mini-dialogues, you are asked to listen, discern and comment. Questions are provided for each dialogue. Discuss the questions after each dialogue.

Dialogue a
- i   What position does Mr Long hold in relation to Miss Bright?
- ii   The scene is Britain. What month do you think it is?
- iii How honest does Mr Long feel that Miss Bright is?
- iv   What information was omitted?

Dialogue b
- i   What was the relationship between Henry and Clara?
- ii   Why did Henry seem so surprised when Clara cancelled their date?
- iii How honest do you think Clara was being? Is there something Henry doesn't know?

Dialogue c
- i   What is the patient's real problem?
- ii   How does the doctor show that he has failed to pick up this problem?
- iii Why doesn't the patient state what his problem is?

Dialogue d
- i   Whom are Mavis and Doris gossiping about?
- ii   What is the unstated subject of their conversation?
- iii What are they hinting at?

Dialogue e
- i   How clear are the appraiser and the appraisee about the purpose of their interview?
- ii   What are the differences in their objectives?

2   Now work in groups to compare your impressions and to give reasons for your conclusions. What do the five mini-dialogues have in common?

D STRUCTURE AND LANGUAGE USAGE (see Study Notes, page 72)

1   Make new sentences from the following, using the supplementary phrases in the correct form but expressing approximately the same meaning.

a   The Board are sorry the company didn't diversify two or three years ago.
   i   The Board wish . . .
   ii The Board regret . . .

b   Jane feels she would have been happier doing a different subject at university.
   i   Jane feels she should . . .
   ii Jane feels she ought . . .
   iii wish

c   I wish I'd worked harder at maths.
   i   If only . . .
   ii I regret . . .

d   The engineer didn't remember to check the pressure gauge.
   i   The engineer failed
   ii forgot
   iii omitted

e   There aren't enough maths teachers.
   i   There/need (noun)
   ii shortage

f   I don't have to come along, do I?
   i   need (verb)
   ii necessary

g   The people at the top don't really understand.
   i   lack (noun)
   ii absence

h   It was an entirely wasted journey for us.
   i   need (verb)
   ii necessary

i   Neither company has won as many orders this year as expected.
   i   shortfall
   ii fall short/expectations

j   We need another two chairs.
   i   short of
   ii short

k It was a waste of time writing to him because I saw him the next day.
  i need (verb)
  ii need (verb)/bother (verb)
l His hair's too long.
  i cutting
  ii do with (colloquial)
m He doesn't seem to have any idea how to manage people.
  i lack (verb)
  ii good at

2 (see Study Notes, page 72)
If you wished to shorten the following sentences, which words could you leave out without changing the meaning?
a Those who were responsible for this will be punished.
b While he was in Cairo he started learning conversational Arabic.
c The government ministers who were involved in these tax scandals were forced to resign.
d This substance, which was discovered entirely by accident, later proved to be a hitherto unknown element.
e He stared at the floor because he was too nervous to reply.
f Although she was already middle-aged, she was still strikingly beautiful.
g Whether it's true or untrue, it shouldn't have been said!
h The poor people and the sick people from the surrounding area used to come to them for help.
i His last request, which was for his son to visit him, was never met.
j On the way up the drive, Watson happened to notice a man who was half hidden by the bushes.
k The main argument of his school of thought, which was that scientific laws have no exceptions, was unacceptable to contemporaries.

3 PASSING THE BUCK

a US President Harry Truman kept a sign on his desk saying 'The buck stops here' meaning that he, the President, had ultimate responsibility and could not pass it to somebody else – as most of us do whenever we can. In the following examples, responsibility for the actions/events has been carefully disguised by the speaker. Discuss how the sentences could be changed so that someone accepts responsibility or someone is clearly held responsible.

Example: We were driving along and suddenly we were rammed by this idiot behind.
= *We pulled up a bit too sharply, causing the car behind to crash into us.*
= *We slowed down to look at a shop window and the car behind hit us.*

    i   Somehow all the glasses got broken. We ....
    ii   Several things have gone missing from this office recently. (colloquial) Employees ....
    iii   It just fell out of my hand!
    iv   We just ran out of road.
    v   We were driving along quite happily and this lunatic came out of a side turning!
    vi   My money's run out!
    vii   This stupid machine won't work!
    viii   It must have got thrown away.
    ix   It must have got mislaid.

b Now reverse the process and make it possible for it to be somebody else's or nobody's fault. The passive with or without 'get' is often very useful in this. Discuss the various possibilities.

Example: I'm terribly sorry, I've broken your glasses.
I'm afraid your glasses got broken.

    i   It's my fault. I put the wrong batteries in.
    ii   We took the bend too fast and hit the back of a Volkswagen that was turning out.
    iii   We're overspending.
    iv   The council has allowed outside developers to alter the whole character of the place.
    v   I'd somehow mixed up all the invoices, causing chaos in the Accounts Office.
    vi   I'm to blame. I took a large pile of envelopes and quite a lot of stamps home.
    vii   We've confused the whole problem now.

PASSIVES (With and without 'Get')

E WRITING ACTIVITY

EXTENSION: 'DON'T REPEAT'

1   It is one of the unwritten rules of attractive style that you should try to avoid constant repetition of, for example, the same noun in a passage by using a variety of nouns or pronouns to take its place. Look at the following news report and notice how many different words are used instead of (a) plane and (b) incident.

BA PLANES WITHIN 50 FT OF DISASTER

Two British Airways jets came within 50 ft of a mid-air collision over Stanmore, Middlesex, when one pilot had to pull his *craft* into a steep climb over *the other*, it was revealed yesterday. The Trade and Industry Secretary is to be questioned about the *incident*.

A report by the Accident Investigation Board reveals that the *near miss* involved a BAC 1-11 from Edinburgh and a Boeing 737 from Munich. Only passengers on the Munich to London *flight* were aware of the *emergency*.

2   TEXT IMPROVEMENT

Rewrite the following text, avoiding repetition of (a) plane (b) crash. The plane involved was a Hercules C-130 transport (not a jet).

An Iranian *plane crashed* in south-western Iran on Friday. Iran's official news agency said the *plane crashed* just before landing owing to technical failure. The *plane* was carrying 91 soldiers and 7 crew when it *crashed* into the side of one of the highest mountains in the area.

3   Write a similar news report describing a near miss between an English sailing-boat and a Dutch fishing vessel in poor visibility off the coast of Kent. Use a variety of ways of referring to the vessels involved (e.g. craft/vessel/sailing boat/the larger ship).

The schooner	**The fishing boat**
UK registered	Dutch registered
200 tonnes	500 tonnes
SS *Bristol*	*Hilversum II*

STUDY NOTES

B1 IMPROVING CONDITIONS

Useful vocabulary for discussion

a poverty; housing; lack of sanitation; work conditions; illiteracy; lack of education; disease; health problems; alcoholism; exploitation; child mortality; death in childbirth

b unemployment; the environment; acid rain; the nuclear issue; terrorism; the economic situation; drugs; AIDS

c to increase public awareness; to get a message across; to influence the government/public opinion; to enlist public support for a cause; to mount a publicity campaign; to lobby MPs; to educate the public; to dislike regulation by outside bodies; right-wingers

d a disinterested love of humanity; to feel dissatisfaction with life as it is; to want to leave the world a better place than you find it; to know what's good for other people; to want gratitude

B2 WHAT'S THE PROBLEM? WHAT'S MISSING?

a *Useful vocabulary for discussion (not in the order of the questions)*

shortcomings; understanding (noun); tact; to do some market research; communication; guilt/guilty; to have business sense; a spirit of co-operation; committee skills; to have thought for others; consultation; 'sharing'; to have consideration; moral courage; to confide in somebody; to feel remorse; to be inconsiderate; to do your 'homework' (e.g. to study the background of someone you are going to interview on television); to take somebody into your confidence

Remedies

to pluck up courage; to show more character; to take people's feelings seriously; to make yourself more aware of others; to go on a training course; to be replaced (e.g. as chairperson); to go on a business management course

b *Useful vocabulary for discussion (not in order of the questions)*

recognition; respect; understanding; consideration; manners; consultation; dependability; humility; sensitivity

c *Useful vocabulary for discussion*

self-sufficient; to cope; to manage; not to mind; to enjoy your own company; to busy yourself; to occupy your mind; 'thinking time'

shifty; shifty-eyed; uneasy; distrustful; to look someone straight in the eye; trust; honesty; to try to hide something

small-talk; to talk for the sake of talking; to rack your brains trying to think of something to say

4
STUDY NOTES

71

4 STUDY NOTES

D1 STRUCTURE AND LANGUAGE USAGE

Study the following examples carefully so that, when you do the exercise, you can apply the information they give on structure.

There's a need for greater medical expertise in the northern region.
I think he will eventually regret not being more open with us.
On checking my change, I found I was £10 short.
He needn't come on the course, need he? (or He doesn't need to come on the course, does he?)
You needn't have bothered to do it just for me!
I wish I'd known you were in London.
We're going to fall short of our target, but only by 5%.
It will be necessary for all personnel to fill in the form.
Somebody should have pointed this out at an earlier stage.
There's a total absence of common sense on the part of the organisers.

D2 STRUCTURE AND LANGUAGE USAGE

Study the following examples and apply the information they give on structures to D2.

a The Personnel Manager gave instructions for all master discs to be kept in the safe.
b Actually we started collecting this kind of painting while in Germany.
c The ministers named in the latest re-shuffle have all visited No.10 today.
d Two old barges, half covered by mud and weeds, lay on the river-bank.
e A special hospital for the physically handicapped is being built just outside the town.
f 'I think it's just wrong-headed!'
   Wrong-headed or not, we've still got to do it.'
g Her brother was a brilliant scientist, although rather arrogant and overbearing.
h These beautiful animals, made extinct by over-hunting, now exist only as museum specimens.
i Those interested should apply to the College Office.
j I found Jane outside, too upset to come in.
k I thought his last proposal, that the whole matter should be shelved until next year, was very suspicious.

5 THE GENERAL AND THE PARTICULAR

Talking about generalizations, stereotypes; relating to other people and groups

A READING TEXTS

1 READING

See Unit 1, Section A (page 5) for instructions. Text B for this unit will be found on page 175.

Text A

THE QUALITIES OF A TEACHER by H C Dent

Here I want to try to give you an answer to the question: What personal qualities are desirable in a teacher? Probably no two people would draw up exactly similar lists, but I think the following would be generally accepted.

First, the teacher's personality should be pleasantly lively and attractive. This does not rule out people who are physically plain, or even ugly, because many such have great personal charm. But it does rule out such types as the over-excitable, melancholy, frigid, sarcastic, cynical, frustrated and over-bearing: I would say too, that it excludes all of dull or purely negative personality. I still stick to what I said in my earlier book: that school children probably 'suffer more from bores than from brutes'.

Secondly, it is not merely desirable but essential for a teacher to have a genuine capacity for sympathy – in the literal meaning of that word; a capacity to tune in to the minds and feelings of other people, especially, since most teachers are school teachers, to the minds and feelings of children. Closely related with this is the capacity to be tolerant – not, indeed, of what is wrong, but of the frailty and immaturity of human nature which induce people, and again especially children, to make mistakes.

Thirdly, I hold it essential for a teacher to be both intellectually and morally honest. This does not mean being a plaster saint. It means that he will be aware of his intellectual strengths, and limitations, and will have thought about and decided upon the moral principles by which his life shall be guided. There is no contradiction in my going on to say that a teacher should be a bit of an actor. That is part of the technique of teaching, which demands that every now and then a teacher should be able to put on an act – to enliven a lesson, correct a fault, or award praise. Children, especially young children, live in a world that is rather larger than life.

A teacher must remain mentally alert. He will not get into the profession if of low intelligence, but it is all too easy, even for people of above-average intelligence, to stagnate intellectually – and that means to deteriorate intellectually. A teacher must be quick to adapt himself to any situation, however improbable (they happen!) and able to improvise, if necessary at less than a moment's notice. (Here I should stress that I use 'he' and 'his' throughout the book simply as a matter of convention and convenience.)

On the other hand, a teacher must be capable of infinite patience. This, I may say, is largely a matter of self-discipline and self-training; we are none of us born like that. He must be pretty resilient; teaching makes great demands on nervous energy. And he should be able to take in his stride the innumerable petty irritations any adult dealing with children has to endure.

Finally, I think a teacher should have the kind of mind which always wants to go on learning. Teaching is a job at which one will never be perfect; there is always something more to learn about it. There are three principal objects of study: the subject, or subjects which the teacher is teaching; the methods by which they can best be taught to the particular pupils in the classes he is teaching; and – by far the most important – the children, young people, or adults to whom they are to be taught. The two cardinal principles of British education today are that education is education of the whole person, and that it is best acquired through full and active co-operation between two persons, the teacher and the learner.

from *Teaching as a Career*, by H. C. Dent, Batsford, 1961

2 QUESTIONS ON THE TEXTS

TEXT A

a   To what extent do you agree with this picture of the ideal teacher? Would you add any qualities or skills?

b   Did your teachers come up to these standards?

TEXTS B AND B1

a   Many of the more 'difficult' students at the school in question come from farming families who have lived on the same land for generations and whose children, only 60 or 70 years ago, might have left school at 12 to work on the farm. Is it perhaps just a waste of time trying to educate them beyond their chosen way of life?

b   How does the great disparity between theory and practice mentioned by both teachers come about and how could it be reduced?

BOTH TEXTS

a   What might be the responses of the authors of Texts B and B1 to Text A?

b   What are the present-day problems in education in your country?

B COMMUNICATIVE ACTIVITIES

1 IDEALS AND ACTUALITIES (see Study Notes, page 87)

a   The authors of Texts B1 and B2 wrote of the way circumstances made it difficult for them to live up to the ideal of a teacher. Discuss what the ideal is in the following cases and then the ways in which circumstances make it difficult to achieve:

   i   policemen   ii   politicians   iii   university students

b   What about you? How do you measure up to your own ideal?

c   What rules do you make for yourself regarding, for example, fitness, food and drink, relationships, or your general behaviour? Do you manage to keep to them?

d   What do *you* do if:
   i   You find £5 in the street. Do you take it to the police station?
   ii   You are given too much change by a shop assistant?
   iii The waiter forgets to put one relatively small item on your restaurant bill?
   iv   The bus conductor forgets to take your fare?

2 THE STATE AND THE INDIVIDUAL
(see Study Notes, page 87)

We may belong to a country, we may have nationality, but exactly what responsibilities and duties does that fact entail? The answer to that question depends very much both on what kind of constitutional and political systems we live under and our own individual interpretation of the demands made on us by that system.

a   Make sure you know the meaning of the following and then discuss how they relate to the rights and duties of the individual with regard to the state.

   i   the Welfare State   vi   religious freedom
   ii   taxation   vii   the rule of law
   iii military service   viii the constitution
   iv   having children   ix   conscientious objectors
   v   patriotism   x   freedom of speech

b   Speaking more personally now, how do you see *your* duties to your country? Discuss everything from feelings to money.

c   Talk about your country's responsibilities towards *you*. What rights do you have? What do you have a right to expect in return for what you give under (b)?

d   In some European countries there are laws against people putting washing out in the garden or cleaning the car on Sundays. In South Korea you can be sent to prison for helping a pupil with homework. Aren't these examples of infringements of personal freedom? Where should we draw the line?

e   Are the activities of the following ever justified?

   i   revolutionaries   iv   deserters
   ii traitors   v   welfare scroungers (colloquial)
   iii terrorists   vi   defectors

3 THE INDIVIDUAL VERSUS THE REST (see Study Notes, page 87)

In recent years, particularly in the US, there has been a lot of interest in assertiveness training, the purpose of which is to regulate human interactions in such a way that each interactant openly expresses his or her *real* needs, and respects those of others, thus avoiding the other possible strategies of aggression, submission and manipulation.

a   Here are four types of interaction posited by this kind of theory. Study them carefully and then decide which of them applies to *you*. Assertiveness training recommends the behaviour described in (iv).

I AGGRESSIVENESS

Being pushy, trying to force people to do things, attacking, blaming, putting others down, not listening, giving orders (rather than requests) when it's inappropriate, deciding for others, over-reacting, reacting to threatening situations by attacking, forcing own point of view, not considering others' point of view.

I'm OK... ...You're not

II BEING MANIPULATIVE OR INDIRECT

'Conning' others into doing things you want them to, being two-faced, appearing to put others up but in fact putting them down, deciding for others without their realising, making veiled threats, insincere ego-boosting, making others feel guilty, attacking in a sly way.

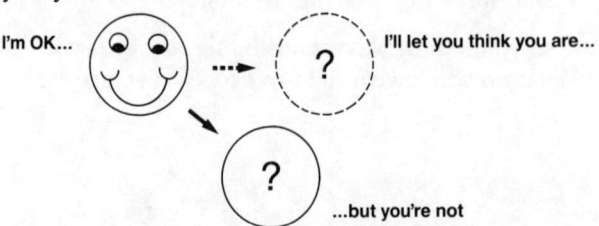

I'm OK...   I'll let you think you are...   ...but you're not

DISCUSSING MODELS OF INTERACTION

III SUBMISSIVENESS

Not saying what you want, going along with others to keep the peace/be liked, agreeing to do things you don't want to do without negotiating, and doing them resentfully/badly/late/not at all, complaining behind the scenes, letting others make the decisions, putting yourself down, being over-apologetic, waffling and not getting to the point, running away from confrontation situations.

I'm not OK... ...You are

IV ASSERTIVENESS

Stating what you want clearly, gently and firmly; acknowledging your own right (and that of others) to state what you want, standing up for yourself and those dependent on you, making your own decisions and allowing others to make theirs, listening to other people's point of view without necessarily going along with it, showing respect for yourself and others, giving praise and constructive criticism, taking responsibility for own feelings and decisions, helping others to be assertive, treating adults as adults.

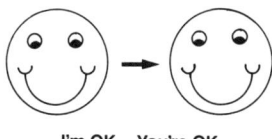

I'm OK... You're OK

b   Which is the worst of the first three categories in your opinion:
    i   for the person himself/herself?
    ii   for people on the receiving end?

c   Have you known people who fitted perfectly into one of the categories (i)–(iv)? Tell the group about them.

d   What, in your opinion, are the long-term effects of types (i) and (iii) behaviour?

e   Can our closest relationships be similarly classified, or is this typology only appropriate to general social relationships?

f   Assertiveness training has often been discussed in relation to feminism. Why is it especially relevant?

g   'Such typologies are simplistic overgeneralisations about the richness and mystery of human interaction.' What do you think?

4 GENERALISATIONS (see Study Notes, page 87)
A STEREOTYPES

Instead of spending time and energy really getting to know the people we come into contact with, most of us take a short cut and slot them into ready-made categories called 'stereotypes'. In this way we disregard their individual qualities and fabricate a similarity to the general category where in fact there may be none.

Here are some UK stereotypes:

i   What mental states are suggested by the stereotypes?

ii   Which physical details in the drawing give clues as to the mental states of the stereotypes?

iii   To what extent do they resemble your stereotypes of the same positions in society?

iv   What would you say were the stereotypes of the following, with regard to physical appearance, mental attitudes and typical behaviour?
– A male tourist from Texas
– an English football fan
– a long-distance truck driver
– a vegetarian conservationist and anti-nuclear pacifist
– a (radical) feminist

v   In the UK the stereotype of the Ford Capri driver is a 'macho probably, working-class young man in his early 20s who imagines he's a racing driver, and is, or thinks he is, attractive to women'. Discuss what part of the following (or other factors you may like to add) play in the maintenance of stereotypes: (a) make of car (b) hairstyles.

B SWEEPING GENERALISATIONS

The following sweeping generalisations have been taken from a very humorous book on marriage called *How to Survive Matrimony* by Herald Froy (Frederick Muller, 1958.)

What wives like
Wives in general are in favour of security, clothes, women's magazines, gossip, royalty, dreams, cage birds, photographs, presents, washing machines, polish, astrology, tea, telephones, babies, boiled sweets, weddings, hairdressers, vicars, Christmas, knitting, supermarkets, funerals, chocolate, television, parks, shoes, ornaments, sherry, cats, lawsuits, colours, happy endings, fresh air, recipes, poodles, mirrors, Paris, money, autumn, eldest boys, poetry, toast, rings, tragedy, whispering, sales, insurance policies, a nice tune, floral patterns, brown paper, having their own way, lovely views, holidays, string, oranges and dieting.

What wives do not like
Drink, secretaries, gold, late nights, other women, gambling, darts, exploring, idleness, cricket, Sunday newspapers, logic, snooker, football, boxing, business lunches, argument, pubs, politics, whistling, universities, insects, abstract art, humour, unexpected guests, sarcasm, chess and mice.

i   Surely some of these generalisations are very true, aren't they? Compare them with your own experiences.

ii What would a (stereotypical) feminist say about these extracts? Would she find them funny?

iii Discuss what should be included in two similar lists of what the average contemporary husband likes/does not like.

DISCUSSING STEREOTYPES AND IMAGES

5 BELONGING (see Study Notes, page 88)

i

ii

iii

iv

v

a   Look at the pictures and discuss what the people who make up each of the groups are called. What is the name of the group they are (or were) part of?

b   Discuss what feelings link the individual members.

c   Talk in a similar way about a group that you have knowledge or direct experience of.

C LISTENING ACTIVITIES

1   Study the photograph of a painting ('The Clergyman's Visit', by Frederic Daniel Hardy) done in 1854. With another member of the class, discuss:

a   what the priority numbers indicate as to the way of life in 1854.

b   whether, and how much, these priorities have changed.

2   The broadcast you are about to hear was made to commemorate the exchange of 50 years of weekly radio programmes between the US and Britain. The broadcaster is welcomed as a scholar and humanist on both sides of the Atlantic.

a   As you listen to the broadcast, make lists of what you consider to be (i) benefits (ii) disasters. Compare your notes with those of other students and give reasons for your conclusions.

b   Listen to the broadcast again, paying attention to implications for present-day life. Then produce your own list of significant events from 1974 until now. Present your list to a group of students and discuss any reasons for the differences.

D STRUCTURE AND LANGUAGE USAGE
(see Study Notes, page 88)

> detail(s)   specifics   idea   technicality   generalities   outline   minutiae
> general terms   gist

1 Complete the sentences below using one of the words in the box above. Give more than one possibility whenever you can.

a The lecturer gave a general overview of the subject but didn't have time to ....

b I am interested in the general principles of law but am bored by ....

c Don't bother to give me a word-for-word account of what he said, just ......

d It was rather disappointing – the panel didn't go into any details but just talked ....

e There's no need to go into great detail at this point, just tell me .... what you're thinking of saying at the meeting.

f I know you haven't got the exact figures, but can you just give me ....

g She did well in the test generally but was failed ....

h Your secretary is quite a perfectionist, isn't she – she pays ....

2 Make three new sentences of similar meaning to the following sentences, using the words given.

a The pattern discovered in one case-history will not necessarily apply generally.
  i applicable   ii generalise   iii generalisations

b Could you provide us with a list of the things you'll be needing?
  i specifying   ii itemise   iii list (verb)

c That's a very good example of exactly the kind of attitude I was describing.
  i illustration   ii illustrate   iii exemplify

d This problem only occurs with engines of this type and year.
  i peculiarity   ii characteristic   iii peculiar

5

3 BECOMING PART OF SOMETHING BIGGER
(see Study Notes, page 88)

| incorporate | merge | swallow up | become part of | integrate |
| assimilate | | | | |

Make at least two new sentences of approximately the same meaning for each of the following examples using vocabulary from the box above.

a   Apparently geography isn't taught as a separate subject any more in the schools – it's ……….. humanities.

b   For a brief moment we glimpsed our quarry silhouetted against the sunset. Then ……….. gathering darkness.

c   For the first 80 years after immigrating these families kept their separate identity, and it is only in the last 20 years ………..

d   General Motors may have taken them over, but it's such an individual firm with lots of character and little idiosyncrasies that it will take a long time ………..

e   When I was born it was a small village separated from Newcastle by miles of green fields, but now ………..

4 FOCUSING ATTENTION (see Study Notes, page 88)

We often use words like 'particularly', 'primarily', 'chiefly', 'principally', 'mainly', 'mostly', 'largely', 'specifically', 'notably', 'simply', 'exclusively' and 'purely' to focus attention on one part of the sentence.
   Complete a second sentence of more or less equivalent meaning for each of the following, using the words in brackets.

Example: Of the several topics I shall be speaking on I will give most attention to the growth of vigilante groups. (I shall ……….. particularly ………..)
= I shall be speaking on several topics particularly on vigilante groups

a   The main reason our products are not selling is that they're overpriced. (Our ……….., primarily ………..)

b   We have itemised the grounds for complaint as poor service, unimaginative menus and overpriced telephone calls. (There were several ……….. principally ………..)

c   Our main reason for not backing it is the expense. (We are unable ……….. principally………..)

d   Our main reason for not tendering for the contract is the time scale involved. (We shall not be ……….. chiefly ………..)

e   The main cause of the accident was negligence on the part of the two signalmen involved. (The accident ……… largely ………)

f   The main consideration in putting back the starting date is to give the new cast members time to settle in. (The opening date ……… principally ………)

5 GENERAL OR PARTICULAR?

The following could be continued so that (i) the whole sentence has a general reference, or (ii) the whole sentence has a relatively more particular reference.

Example: The dog is . . .   (i) said to be man's best friend.
(ii) slowly falling asleep.

Suggest similar pairs of sentences for the following:

a   A man is . . .   i   The poor . . .
b   The mind . . .   j   Intelligence . . .
c   The painter . . .   k   Scientists . . .
d   The aeroplane . . .   l   A painter . . .
e   A horse has . . .   m   An aeroplane . . .
f   A helicopter . . .   n   The horse . . .
g   The evening . . .   o   The helicopter . . .
h   Racism is . . .

E WRITING ACTIVITY

1

Write a short essay (minimum 300 words) on the problems of either secondary or university education in your country.

2

Refer to section B 3 on assertiveness training.
Write a short account (minimum 60 words) of what assertiveness training tries to discourage on the one hand and encourage on the other.

3 FOCUSING ATTENTION (see Study Notes, page 88)

After working on the Study Notes, write a completely new sentence of approximately the same meaning, including the items in brackets, for each of the following:

a   All I'm saying is that it isn't a particularly new idea. (I'm simply ....)

b   My only reason for going there is to consult one of the researchers. (I'm .... specifically ....)

c   The only reason I'm turning it down is the absurdly low salary. (I'm .... solely ....)

d   Should you turn it down just on that account? (alone)

e   I suppose there are other reasons as well. (not simply)

f   As far as I'm concerned, convenience is the prime consideration. (purely .... matter)

g   Only certain retail outlets will stock them. (They .... exclusively .... available ....)

h   'Man cannot live by bread alone'. ('Bread', remember is used *metaphorically* here.) (solely or exclusively)

4 DIFFICULT PLURALS (see Study Notes, page 88)

a   Check the meanings of all the following words.

b   Look carefully at the Study Notes on page 88. Apply the same 'rules' to the items below and complete the list.

Singular	Plural	Singular	Plural
basis	....	...........*	genera
....	cacti	synopsis	....
lay-by	....	assistant treasurer	....
hypothesis	....	curriculum	....
		passer-by*	
hero	....	....	analyses
....	geese	veto	....
stratum	....	medium	mediums or...........
....	diagnoses	locus	....
criterion	....	syllabus	syllabuses or...........
woman doctor*	....	thesis	....
gin-and-tonic	....	....	stimuli
memorandum	....	mother-in-law*	....
close-up	....	nucleus	nucleuses or...........
....	radiuses or...........		

c   Make sentences using between five and eight plurals you were not sure of before.

STUDY NOTES

B1 IDEALS AND ACTUALITIES

Useful vocabulary for discussion

a i A policeman should be fair; unprejudiced; calm; with plenty of self-control; the kind of person you respect.
 ii disinterested; wanting to promote the welfare of others (rather than 'line his own pockets' (colloquial)
 iii He or she ought to be hardworking; intellectually curious; with wide intellectual and cultural interests.
b I'm not very good . . . in that I don't . . .; My problem is that . . .; I don't always . . .; I suppose I should be more . . .
c I promised myself I'd . . .; I'm not supposed to . . .; I try to . . .
d I report it to the police; I mention it to him.

B2 THE STATE AND THE INDIVIDUAL

Useful vocabulary for discussion

a (i) support (verb and noun) 'a safety-net', sickness/unemployment benefit
 (iv) the citizens of the future (vi) loyalty to worship in our own way (vii) no one is above the law (viii) the embodiment of the basic principles and laws of a nation (ix) the dictates of conscience (x) the public expression of opinion, freedom to express your opinions.
b obey; comply with laws etc.; enhance its reputation in the eyes of foreigners; to defend
c military protection; security; basic necessities
d interfere in; regulate; should not concern itself with . . .
e 'The end justifies the means'; What else can?; There may be no other way to . . . a loyalty to a 'higher' cause/a different ideology

B3 THE INDIVIDUAL VERSUS THE REST

Useful vocabulary for discussion

b By far the worst is . . . The worst type in my opinion is . . . He's his own worst enemy (= his behaviour makes life difficult for him)
c That's *exactly* like . . .; That's just how my father behaves . . .; My boss is like that . . .!
d resentment; alienation; retaliation
f a male-dominated society; a male-oriented society
g simplistic; oversimplified; they don't take into account the . . .; they totally ignore . . .

B4 GENERALISATIONS

Useful vocabulary for discussion

kindly (adj.), bossy, simple-minded
the way (s)he stands/sits/glares/folds his (her) legs
It's his walk/expression/look/hair
I can tell from his expression that he's . . .

B5 BELONGING

useful vocabulary for discussion

b comradeship, devotion to the same ideals, team spirit, a feeling of loyalty to the group

D1 STRUCTURE AND LANGUAGE USAGE

Study the way the words in *italics* are used before completing the exercise.

It's no good *talking in generalities* – what we need is to *go into quite a lot of detail*, even at this stage. If we negotiate the arrangement *in general terms*, the legal department can sort out *the minutiae*. The gist of what she said is that she's not interested. Could you give me *a rough idea* about the weekend? The horse that came in first was disqualified *on a technicality*. You'll have to *pay more attention to detail in* your new job! They've informed us *in outline* of their plans.

D2 Before attempting D2 and D3, check with the help of a good dictionary that you know not only the meaning but also *how to use* the following:
to apply to; to be applicable to; to generalise from; to make generalisations from; to specify; to itemise; to list; an illustration of (example); to illustrate (= give an example of); to exemplify; to be a peculiarity/characteristic of; to be peculiar to

D3 to assimilate; incorporate; integrate; merge; swallow up

D4 FOCUSING ATTENTION

(Instructions are as for D1 and D2 above.)
particularly; primarily; principally; specifically; mostly; mainly; chiefly; largely

E3 FOCUSING ATTENTION

Look carefully at the way the words in *italics* are used before attempting E3.

In my opinion they're *simply* saying it isn't on. Surely this is *purely* a matter for the Prime Minister and the Cabinet?
I think you're doing it *solely* to improve the look of your CV! I wouldn't do it for that reason *alone*. I'm sorry, sir, this clubhouse is *exclusively* for the use of members. Did he resign *solely* as a result of that disagreement? My father had it *specially* made by a local cabinet-maker.

E4 DIFFICULT PLURALS

Study the following carefully before attempting E4. Then apply same 'rules' to the examples in the exercise, remembering that those marked with an asterisk (*) are exceptions.

phenome*non* → phenome*na*;   take-off → take-offs;   cri*sis* → cri*ses*;
memorand*um* → memorand*a*;   toma*to* → toma*toes*;   t*oo*th → t*ee*th;
stimul*us* → stimul*i*;   *genus → genera;   *mother-in-law → mothers-in-law;
*woman doctor → women doctors;   *passer-by → passers-by;
rum-and-coke → rum-and-cokes.

6 STANDPOINT
Discussing opinions, beliefs and ideologies

A READING TEXTS

1 READING

See Unit 1, Section A (page 5) for instructions. Text B for this unit will be found on page 177.

Text A

THE ELEMENTS OF POLITICAL CONFLICT
by Maurice Duverger

In all human communities, and even in animal societies, power confers certain advantages and privileges, such as honour, prestige, material benefits and pleasures. As a result, there is a bitter struggle for power, taking place on two different planes. The first, which could be called *horizontal*, opposes man to man, group to group, or class to class, in the struggle to attain, share or influence power. Individuals compete for a parliamentary seat, an appointment as prefect, a ministerial portfolio, the general's insignia, a cardinal's hat. In large communities these individual conflicts are paralleled by group rivalries within the society, whether parish, regional or national, by conflicts of class, race and ideology.

The second type of political conflict takes place on a *vertical* plane, opposing power, the government which commands, to the citizens who resist, the rulers to the ruled, the members of the community to the whole apparatus of social control. Not that the opposition is between the citizens on one side and an abstract 'power' on the other; rather, it is between some citizens, who hold power, and others, who are subject to it. Power always works to the benefit of one group, one clan, one class; the opposition to it comes from other groups, clans, classes, who wish to take the place of those in power. Nevertheless, within the dominant class there is a minority which controls the apparatus of government, and between this minority and the majority of the ruling class there arise conflicts which are quite distinct from the clashes between the ruling class and the rest of the population. These divergences between rulers and ruled, between those who command and those who must obey, between the holders of power and the other citizens, can be seen in all human society.

The various political ideologies differ not only in the relative importance they give to conflict and integration but also in their conception of the conflict and its causes. For Marxists, political disagreement is caused by the socio-economic structures. The modes of production, such as ancient or medieval agriculture, or modern industry, are determined by the state of technical development, and in their turn they give rise to social classes, which either rule or are ruled, and therefore conflict. The ruling classes use the state to maintain their power over the other classes, which naturally resist. Political strife thus reflects the class struggle, and is therefore essentially collective, setting group against group, within the community. Competition between individuals is only of secondary importance to Marxists, who also neglect the clash between citizens and state, except in so far as it coincides with the conflict between the dominated classes and the dominant class which rules the state. However, the experience of Stalinism has made them aware of the problem.

Liberal philosophies, on the other hand, mainly consider the other two forms of political strife, that is, competition between individuals to obtain the best position in society, and the struggles of citizens against power, which is by nature oppressive. Western thinkers hold that both these forms of strife are caused by factors which are essentially psychological. Power corrupts because it allows those who rule to indulge their passions to the detriment of those they rule over. 'All power corrupts and absolute power corrupts absolutely.' Power is a permanent temptation, and as Alain says, 'there is no man who, if he had total power, and were quite free to use it, would not sacrifice justice to his passions'. Furthermore, in a society where needs outstrip the goods available to satisfy them, every man strives to obtain for himself the maximum advantage over his fellows, and holding power is an effective means to this end. This elementary psychological portrait of *homo politicus*, motivated like *homo economicus* by personal interest, is today being enriched and complicated by the findings of psychoanalysis, which attributes more complex motivational forces to political strife.

Maurice Duverger, *The Idea of Politics*, Methuen, 1966

QUESTIONS ON THE TEXTS

TEXT A

a How far do you agree with the following quotations used by Professor Duverger?

   i 'All power corrupts and absolute power corrupts absolutely'
   ii 'There is no man who, if he had total power and were quite free to use it, would not sacrifice justice to his passions'

b If you think it is to some extent true, describe how the process of corruption takes place.

TEXT B

a To what extent do you consider Russell's ideas, as expressed here, realistic?

b Would you describe Russell on the evidence of this text as a 'liberal'? Justify your opinion.

BOTH TEXTS

a   How would you describe the different approaches of the two writers?

b   To what extent do you think the elements considered in Text A contribute to the problems outlined in Text B?

B   COMMUNICATIVE ACTIVITIES

1   POLITICAL BELIEFS AND ISSUES (see Study Notes, page 104)

liberal   right-wing   radical   conservative   social democratic

a   Can you match these labels with the description of different political beliefs below?

   i   You emphasise the value of the family and of people accepting responsibility for their own well-being rather than expecting the state to look after you.

   ii Your political opinions may be 'right' or 'left', but in either case you feel that very fundamental changes are necessary if society is to be put on the right lines.

   iii You favour a political movement that advocates transition from a capitalistic society to a (more) socialist one by gradual, peaceful and democratic means.

   iv Your beliefs and attitudes are extremely conservative and perhaps nationalistic. 'Authority', 'self-discipline' and 'independence' are important concepts to you.

   v   You have a strong belief in individual freedom, less government control, and in the essential goodness of human beings.

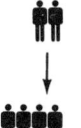

b   In what ways do political parties on the left and on the right of the political spectrum traditionally differ in their approach to the following issues?

   i   taxes
   ii   education
   iii law and order
   iv   defence
   v   public ownership versus privatisation
   vi   sexual equality

c   What typical criticisms might the following make of each other?

   i   liberals – right-wingers
   ii   communists – socialists
   iii Republicans (USA) – Democrats (USA)

TALKING ABOUT POLITICAL BELIEFS AND ISSUES

d   Political opinions/beliefs are influenced by the economic situation of the country, by personalities and by the media. Discuss how political opinions are:
  i   formed
  ii   changed
  iii gauged
  iv   disappointed

e   Can you say how the items in *italics* relate to the theme of the unit? Think about them in terms of point of view, attitudes, beliefs etc.
  i   A *lobby* (e.g. the gun lobby in the USA) or a *pressure group*.
  ii   The NUM (National Union of Mineworkers) has always been one of the more *militant* unions.
  iii 'We have no right to make any changes until there's a *consensus* in favour of change.'
  iv   They're very *middle-of-the road*.
  v   Having been to public school and Oxbridge, his attitudes started off as rather *elitist* . . .

2 PREJUDICE AND DISCRIMINATION (see Study Notes, page 104)

a   Some academic discussions of prejudice have argued that it is evidence of a seriously flawed personality. Others maintain that it merely represents an extreme case of a necessary mental process we all operate all the time – that of selecting from, classifying and predicting experience so that we can learn from what happens to us, organise our thoughts and make decisions.
  i   Where do prejudices come from? From our parents? From our education? From our cultural environment? From friends? Or are they from somewhere *inside* ourselves?
  ii   When we talk of 'prejudice', we often think immediately of prejudice on grounds of race or colour. What other kinds are there?
  iii Which people in your own country are the victims of prejudices on the following grounds: dress, language or dialect, place of origin, occupation? Discuss this with a partner and then with the whole group.
  iv   To what extent do you think prejudice is attributable to a flawed personality and to what extent is it a normal human attribute?

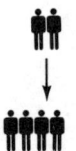

b   How do the following experience other people's prejudice?
  i   older people who have never married
  ii   ethnic minorities

- iii the mentally and physically handicapped
- iv people over 70
- v people who are overweight
- vi gays

c Do *you* feel prejudiced towards any of the above?

BUT WHERE DO WE DRAW THE LINE? (see Study Notes, page 104)

d Do you agree that all the following are examples of prejudice? Some of them have special names. Can you give them?

- i Pat is a convinced feminist. She has found from bitter experience that men are in the main less sensitive than women and less in touch with life.
- ii When Marjorie goes out socially with her workmates, if she asks for orange juice or a Coke, they always try to persuade her to have something stronger (i.e., alcoholic).
- iii Gerald is forty. He lives close to his work and within walking distance of the city centre. Rather than own a car, he prefers to spend his money on foreign travel and frequent trips to London. He doesn't like car-travel, but all his friends and relatives keep getting on at him to buy a car.
- iv It's normal practice in the advertising agency for all job applications from people over 45 to be thrown immediately into the waste-paper basket, even though no age limit is mentioned in their adverts.
- v Bill has turned down some very well-qualified Asian applicants – according to him, this is not because he's prejudiced against them or thinks they wouldn't do the job well, but simply because they wouldn't fit in with the rest of the workforce as well as a white applicant.
- vi The other drivers at the bus depot admit to being prejudiced against the two female bus drivers: they firmly believe that driving buses, because of the physical aspect of their work as well as the potential problem of unruly or violent passengers, makes it a man's job.

DEFINING PREJUDICES AND DISCRIMINATION

e Is the following complaint justified, in your opinion?

> Dear Editor
>
> I was very angry to read the poem 'Rainfall' by Carol Lang which uses the racist word 'blackened' twice, the context making the word to mean 'dirtied'. As a black woman, language is used as a tool against my sisters and me, but I expect more from you with your Black histories, coverage of Black topics etc.
>
> Mary

3 ADJUSTING OUR LANGUAGE OR PERSONALITY
(see Study Notes, page 105)

LANGUAGE

We find that we make adjustments to our language according to the people we are talking to: an extreme illustration of this is the grocer who said that when a woman asked him for back bacon (the best) he called her 'Madam' and when she asked him for streaky (the cheapest) he called her 'Dear'.

Here is a striking example, from early this century, of what happens when we don't adjust:

> The little girl sat down at the table, turned to her hostess and said:
> 'I see you keep your house very clean. Cleanliness is next to godliness, you know.'
> The lady smiled and looked at her husband.
> 'Is your husband working?' asked the girl.
> 'But of course!' said the lady. 'What an odd question for you to ask.'
> 'And are you both keeping off the drink?'
> 'What an impertinent little girl!' said the magistrate's wife. 'When you are out visiting you should behave like a lady, my child.'
> 'But I do!' said the little girl. 'When the ladies visit our house, they always ask those questions!'

a Think of the kinds of adjustments you make every day (for example, I say 'Hello' to some people and 'Good morning' to others). Is your language at work different from your language at home, and does it vary with different groups of friends?

b What are the factors that necessitate the adjustment? Are they connected with the degree of familiarity in your relationship, for example? Or is social position important?

c Discuss how a greeting such as 'Good morning' and an offer such as 'Would you like a cup of coffee?' might change according to which of the following are involved:

- i very close relative or friend
- ii a work colleague of yours in a similar position to you who you know quite well
- iii an important visitor at work you have previously only talked to on the phone

d Think of an *invitation*, a *request*, and an *enquiry* and suggest how they might change according to whether you know the people:
- i very well indeed
- ii quite well
- iii not at all

PERSONALITY

Three images of Churchill

MAKING REQUESTS; ENQUIRIES AND INVITATIONS

a Are you a different person in the eyes of different people? Are you the same person at home as at work? Why is there a difference?

b How do these differences in other people's perceptions of you come about? Is it because of them or because of you?

c How do different people bring out different sides of our personality? Can you give examples from your own experience?

d The following all relate to the way people interact. Say what the problem is (i) from the point of view of the language used and (ii) in relation to the speaker's personality.

i 'I can't make Robert out.'
'Nor can I, really.'
'The thing is, he's *trying to be all things to all men*.'

ii 'I'm sorry, but I think she's *two-faced*.'

iii 'The Managing Director was pretty *patronising*, as usual.'

iv 'Didn't *make any allowances* for your English, did he?'

v '. . . a bit *schoolmistressy*'

vi 'What I like about Barbara is the way she's always so *natural*.'

vii 'Never quite *know where I am* with Mark.'
'Nor do I.'

viii 'Couldn't *get a word in edgeways*. She talks *at* you, doesn't she?'

ix (Young guest to Mayoress at Town Hall reception)
'How are we doing then, me ole darling?'
'I beg your pardon!!'

4 POINTS OF VIEW IN POETRY (see Study Notes, page 106)

Africa's Plea

I am not you –
but you will not
give me a chance,
will not let me be ME.

If I were you –
but you know
I am not you
yet you will not
let me be me.

You meddle, interfere
in my affairs
as if they were yours
and you were me.

You are unfair, unwise
foolish to think
that I can be you
talk, act
and think like you.

God made me *me*
He made you *you*
For God's sake
Let me be *me*.

Roland Tombekai Dempster

a   Explain the meaning of the poem, relating it to economics, education, language and lifestyle.

b   Fast food, TV soaps, the obsession with physical fitness – some British people complain that US influence is too great. Has your country experienced this kind of influence by another?

5 ARGUMENT BY POSTCARD AND POSTER

Points of view can also be expressed by means of posters and postcards. Look at the following and discuss which points of view are being expressed. Which do you find yourself in agreement with?

a

b

c

C LISTENING ACTIVITIES

1   You are about to hear a series of words which tend to be emotive and open to personal interpretations. As soon as you hear a word, jot down your first reaction using a descriptive word or phrase. When you have done this, compare your reactions with a group of fellow students and discuss why the reactions might be different. There are no right or wrong responses.

2   Study the following questions *before* you listen to the broadcast:
a   What is the subject of the broadcast?
b   What are the symptoms of the particular illness?
c   For which age group is it more likely to have serious consequences? Why?
d   Why do you think teachers are in favour of a change in the date of examinations?
e   Why is Mr Giles opposed to orthodox chemists' remedies?
f   What is his point of view on the best treatment? How far would you agree with him?

3   a   Now listen to the broadcast. Make short notes if you find it helpful.
    b   Compare and discuss your responses with other students and listen to the broadcast again if necessary.

4 FURTHER DISCUSSION

What is your point of view on:
a   'natural' remedies as opposed to conventional prescriptions?
b   how students can be disadvantaged when sitting examinations?

D STRUCTURE AND LANGUAGE USAGE

1 THE LANGUAGE OF OPINION (see Study Notes, page 106)

Make new sentences, using the items given in an appropriate form:

a The Board consider the changes indispensable.
   i view (noun)   ii convinced   iii see

b But nobody's asked us what *we* think of them!
   i attitude   ii opinion   iii consult

c To me it's just another cost-cutting exercise.
   i opinion   ii concerned   iii regard

d We take the strongest possible exception to the broadcasting of such material at the peak family viewing time. (letter to newspaper)
   i protest (verb)   ii condemn   iii object (verb)

e We suggest it is up to the international community to express its abhorrence of this kind of regime. (letter to newspaper)
   i condemnation   ii denounce   iii revulsion

f These people are parasites! They do nothing themselves but spend all their time criticising other people's efforts!
   i disparage   ii scornful   iii knock (colloquial)

g Bob Geldof's attempts to do something for famine victims deserve our admiration. (letter to newspaper)
   i earn/respect   ii applaud

h I have always been against the present government's education policy, in particular its position on student grants.
   i disagree   ii disapprove   iii disagreement   iv critical

i We wish in the strongest terms to protest at the use of live animals in scientific experiments. (letter to newspaper)
   i register/disapproval   ii condemn

j I'm sorry, but we will not be treated like second-class citizens! (public meeting)
   i object   ii take exception   iii allow

EXPRESSING OPINIONS, APPROVING, DISAPPROVING

2 YOU MIGHT HAVE MENTIONED IT EARLIER! (see Study Notes, page 106)

Look at the following situations and then make new sentences with the verbs below (making any necessary changes), expressing the appropriate feeling or point of view.

a   A friend had arranged to meet you at a certain time but didn't turn up. It would have been possible to phone you, and you want to express your irritation at his not phoning.

   i   might   ii   should   iii   could

b   Your brother Tom said something very unkind about your parents at Christmas. You think it was wrong of him and want him to know how you feel.

   i   need   ii   should   iii   could

c   A junior colleague of yours still hasn't completed a project, even though he promised to have it ready by today.

   i   supposed   ii   should   iii   'are to'

d   A colleague of yours, Anne, is too shy to talk to her boss about a problem at work. She always gets other people to mention the matter for her, which you find rather irritating. You are talking about her to a third person.

   i   will   ii   wish   iii   ought

e   A friend has asked you for help in a rather difficult situation that you don't feel at all qualified or able to help with. You are discussing the problem with your partner.

   i   supposed   ii   can   iii   wish

f   Your wife or husband has made a provisional arrangement for a relative whose company you cannot stand to spend next weekend with you, when you had planned something else.

   i   have to   ii   would   iii   must

3 DISCUSSION (see Study Notes, page 106)

Discuss possible ways of completing the following:

a   As we see it . . .

b   His position is that . . .

c   To me . . .

d   From our point of view . . .

e   The way I see it . . .

f   I hardly need persuading that . . .

MIGHT, SHOULD, COULD, NEED, SUPPOSED TO WISH, OUGHT, WILL, CAN, MUST

E WRITING ACTIVITIES

1 Look back at Section B2. In a short composition (minimum 300 words) discuss whether you consider racial prejudice to be a permanent and ineradicable aspect of human nature or whether it can be eliminated, for example by education.

2 EXTENSION: LETTERS TO THE EDITOR (see Study Notes, page 107)

During 1985–6 there was a prolonged period of industrial action in British schools, which caused a great deal of disruption and aroused very strong feelings in the country as a whole. Here is an example of a letter written to a newspaper during that time:

Dear Sir,

Letter text	Annotations
How sick and tired I am of hearing about the cruel working conditions of teachers!	Aggressive tone / Sarcasm
Poor little dears – how my heart bleeds for them as they try to work out what to do for their twelve weeks plus of holidays!	Patronising tone / Sarcasm
They should have my job and have to start at 6.50 am for 40 weeks of the year and a two-week annual holiday if I'm lucky!	Self-pity
If teachers worked half as hard as other people instead of pussy-footing about between 9.30 and 4 for only ¾ of the year,	Insulting / Exaggeration
the youth of this once-great country wouldn't be the loud-mouthed little louts most of them are! And if their job is so unbearable why aren't they man enough to take themselves off and do something else?	Insulting / Exaggeration / Aggressive tone
I'll tell you why – It's because they've got it easy but they don't know when they're well off!!	Patronising tone

Imagine you are a schoolteacher reading this letter. You feel you have to write a letter to the newspaper in reply, but you wish to avoid the sarcasm, patronising tone, self-pity, etc. of the first letter. Write your reply, calmly defending teachers from this attack. The following points may be useful:

a   A lot of what should be holiday-time is in fact taken up with preparing teaching materials for the next academic year, reading examination set books, and escorting students on educational trips.

b   School-work doesn't stop at four o'clock. Many late afternoons and evenings are taken up with meetings, in-service training, parents' evenings, as well as marking and lesson preparation.

c   A lot of teachers trained for the profession when it was, relatively speaking, much better paid. Since that time other comparable professions have gone ahead in terms of income.

d   Teaching is a mentally and physically exhausting job, although most people don't realise this.

e   The major influence on school-children's behaviour is not schoolteachers but parents.

STUDY NOTES

B1   POLITICAL BELIEFS AND ISSUES

Useful language for discussion

b   Low/high levels of taxation . . . stress the importance of . . . they take the view that . . . they maintain/believe . . . In their view/opinion . . . to them, education/defence is an absolute priority . . . make generous financial provision for . . . accountability of police forces to the local community . . . anti-nuclear arguments . . privatisation increases efficiency . . . the discipline of market forces . . . traditional values . . . a woman's place is in the home . . .

c
  i   to be 'soft' (= too lenient) on such issues as law and order . . . too idealistic/unrealistic . . .
  ii   too reactionary, unenlightened, totalitarian, authoritarian . . . the gradual approach believes in a 'mixed' economy (socialist and capitalist)
  iii welfare . . . big business

d
  iii gauged (= measured) using opinion polls (e.g. Mori/Gallup polls) on cross-sections of people
  ii, iv   loss of ideals
  iv   political scandals

e
  i   to influence public opinion . . . to get favourable publicity for . . .
  ii   to pursue aims aggressively, to follow a policy of confrontation
  iv   . . . avoiding both extremes, tending to neither extreme, disliking extremes . . . moderate

B2   PREJUDICE AND DISCRIMINATION

Prejudice is, literally, 'pre-judging'. A prejudiced person is someone who holds views, often unfair, which are not based on accurate knowledge.

If there are any words you are unsure of in the text or these notes, consult your dictionary. For example, how would you explain what a flawed personality is?

Useful language

    i   It's partly because .../a result of .../Part of the problem is that ...
To some extent it comes from ... Prejudices are often communicated/inculcated/transmitted by ... In some ways/cases they can be seen/regarded as a 'defensive reaction' to a situation ...

    ii   ageism, sexism, class-consciousness, nationalism

    iii   People regard them as ... They're considered to be ... They're treated as second-class citizens ... discriminated against by ...
People from ... are regarded as slow/money-minded/ lazy/... treated as if they are inadequate. We always make jokes about ...
We always poked fun (= made fun) at people who came from ...

    iv   ... it's a result of ... it's a reaction to ... it's part of growing up ... Prejudices are produced by ...

c   I'm slightly prejudiced against ... I'm aware of some prejudice towards ... I admit I'm prejudiced regarding ...

d   Look again at the definition of prejudice in B2 above.

Useful language

Freedom of choice ... up to him/her to decide ... The right to choose ... to yield/give in to social pressures ... to be the same as everyone else ... to conform ... to go along with the crowd .. to be pressurised into doing something ...

e   It's going a bit too far ... It's a bit over the top (colloquial).
She's being oversensitive/hypersensitive.
She's right to object ... She's quite justified.

B3 ADJUSTING OUR LANGUAGE OR PERSONALITY

c   Think of the situations in which we might use these:

Here! Come here! Can you come over here? Could you come over here, please? Would you mind coming over here, please?

Personality: Useful language

b   In the eyes of my employees I'm a monster ... My wife sees me as ... and to my children I'm ... At work I'm always conscious of my position whereas at home ...
... They've got certain pre-conceptions about you ... You have to give an impression of ... ... brings out my competitive/serious/pleasure-loving side ...

d   to try to please everybody ... to say what people want to hear ... to seek popularity ... to talk down to people ... to be bossy ... just to be yourself ... to be unselfconscious ... not to know what somebody is thinking ... to be over-familiar with someone ... to chat somebody up (colloquial)

6

STUDY NOTES

B4 POINTS OF VIEW IN POETRY

Useful language

preserve traditional ways of life/values . . . maintain a separate identity . . . multi-nationals . . . cultural colonialism . . . allow us to be ourselves . . . to develop in our own way . . . sphere of political influence . . . the transmission of Western values by means of TV, films, videos etc. . . . to lose our cultural identity . . . to be left to develop in our own way

D1 THE LANGUAGE OF OPINION

Make sure you know not only the meaning of the following expressions but also how to use them:
to protest at (against), to condemn, to object to, to denounce, to regard, to consult, to be convinced that, to see (= regard), to disparage, to knock (colloquial) (= criticise), to applaud, to disagree, to disapprove of, to be critical of, to be in disagreement with, to earn the respect of, to be scornful of, to express condemnation of/your revulsion against, as far as they are concerned . . . In her view . . . to register our disapproval of . . . to take exception to . . .

D2 YOU MIGHT HAVE MENTIONED IT EARLIER!

Study the following and think of the feeling being expressed. (Consider whether it is CRITICISM, IRRITATION, PERPLEXITY etc.)

Those children *shouldn't have behaved* like that!
Jim *needn't have seemed* so ungrateful.
They *might have given* us a lift home, they were coming this way!
The party *was supposed to have been held* today.
You *could have been* a bit more helpful – they were very kind to us!
I (do) *wish they wouldn't make* so much noise!
Jane *will always leave* the washing-up until the next morning!
I *wish they hadn't given* me the job!
The phone *would ring* just as I'm getting into the bath!
Do you have to make such a dreadful noise!
Must you whistle!
You *ought to discuss that* with your solicitor.
I know it's difficult, but what on earth *can we do*?
'They need you.' But how are we *supposed to help*?

D3 DISCUSSION

Study how the words in *italics* are used in the examples.
The way we see it we've still got a long way to go. (= a lot of work to do, a lot of progress to make)
From the point of view of the company, this is an excellent project with loads (colloquial) of potential.
'Of course *we won't need persuading* that it's worth our while to accept.' (= it is *so clearly* worthwhile)
To me it's all a bit phoney. (colloquial) (= false)
As I see it, there are only two possibilities.

E2   EXTENSION: LETTERS TO THE EDITOR

Useful (reasonable) language for the letter

I'm sorry you should have such a low opinion of my profession but . . . What you should bear in mind is . . . What some non-teachers don't realise is . . . People who haven't done any teaching themselves don't always realise . . . There are a lot of myths about . . .

6 STUDY NOTES

7 IN THE NEGATIVE

Talking about success and failure; ways of saying no

A READING TEXTS

1 READING

See Unit 1, Section A (page 5) for instructions. Text B for this unit will be found on page 179.

Text A

SECRECY IN BRITAIN by Clive Ponting

Secrecy is at the heart of the way in which Whitehall works. We have already seen how Whitehall resembles a small village community, introverted, with its own set of values. This attitude is reinforced by the wall of secrecy around Whitehall. Secrecy makes Whitehall even more inward-looking and ready to argue that 'policy-making' should be restricted to the small group of insiders who have access to all the best information. People outside the magic circle need not be involved because they do not see the really important information kept inside Whitehall, and the public at large is not to be trusted with this information. Instead, Whitehall issues a large amount of publicity material, government statements, White Papers and background documents which mask the real level of secrecy. This is not 'information', it is public relations material designed to back up the political interests of the government. It is of no benefit to the government to provide genuine information, particularly if this could be the basis for real detailed criticism. Governments only publish information that supports what they want to do. Even the monthly and annual sets of statistics that have to be published are doctored as much as possible. All of this is backed up by a compliant news media fed by a well-oiled Government machine and largely content to play by the rules set by Whitehall.

The Official Secrets Act
The legal basis for all government secrecy in this country is the Official Secrets Act, and in particular Section 2 of that Act.

Section 2 of the 1911 Act makes it a criminal offence, punishable with up to two years in prison, for any Crown Servant to pass any piece of information to an 'unauthorised person'. There are other provisions making it an offence to receive the information. The important part of this section is that it not only covers 'classified' or 'secret' information, as many people believe; it involves every single piece of information inside Whitehall. It is therefore a criminal offence to give anybody outside Whitehall any information about what goes on inside the government machine.

Obviously government could not continue to function if the Act was applied rigorously, and there is an exception to the general non-release of information. Disclosure is acceptable when it is 'authorised'. What this actually means is far from clear. Many people might think that in a bureaucratic world like Whitehall there must be a form which is filled in and sent up through the machine for signature at the appropriate level, and the release of information is then 'authorised'. There is no such procedure.

In practice what happens is that Ministers, at the top of the machine, authorise themselves to release whatever information they like, including material classified Confidential and Secret. We shall see that this process is at the heart of the 'lobby system' where Ministers feel free to tell journalists what went on inside the Cabinet room. In practice senior civil servants and others in the upper echelons of Whitehall also feel free to tell the media highly selected items of information from inside the machine. Occasionally they step over the (unmarked) line – for example Admiral Sir Henry Leach's public attack in 1981 on the government for cutting the Royal Navy whilst he was still First Sea Lord. But people at this level are too powerful to suffer more than a light rap over the knuckles. Only when a less powerful civil servant 'leaks' information embarrassing to the government is there a prosecution under the Official Secrets Act.

The Official Secrets Act is therefore a very convenient tool. It enables Whitehall to keep secret all the pieces of information that might damage the government or reveal what really happens inside the machine, whilst also enabling it to deliberately 'leak' a large amount of highly slanted and tendentious material that backs up the general public relations effort.

Inevitably, the system is regularly abused. Secrecy is used not to protect national security but to prevent political embarrassment; and papers that show the fallibility of government policy or the deviousness or duplicity of Ministers can be, and frequently are, highly classified. For example an internal DHSS paper in 1985 on how to cut £120 million a year from the poorest people claiming Supplementary Benefit, how to get the proposals through the independent Social Security Advisory Committee without advance warning, how to start a campaign to 'reduce public expectations and prepare the way for a more restricted social aid scheme' despite the fact that the Minister, Norman Fowler, had earlier pledged that there would be no cash losses, was classified 'secret'. Although the political embarrassment involved is obvious, it is difficult to see how disclosure would cause 'serious injury to the interests of the nation'.

The weight of classified information inside Whitehall provides another effect rather like tunnel vision. Because the information is classified it is seen as more important and reliable than information from outside the machine. This can have disastrous consequences in intelligence assessment but also in every other field where it warps the decision-making process and leads to poor decisions based on inadequate and bad information. A subsidiary consequence is that it increases the self-esteem of those inside the system. Because they have access to this information that seems to be so special they come to see themselves as important people in privileged positions.

from Clive Ponting, *Whitehall: Tragedy and Farce*, Sphere, 1986

2 QUESTIONS ON THE TEXTS

TEXT A

a   Surely civil servants or government employees should expect to have to maintain a high degree of confidentiality because it is essential to efficient government?

b   Similarly, isn't it perfectly understandable that a government should need to produce 'public relations material' rather than 'genuine information' in order to support its policies?

c   How does this degree of secrecy, in Clive Ponting's words, 'warp the decision-making process'?

d   Suggest approximately ten items of vocabulary with a negative or critical colouring that are used by the author in his discussion of UK government secrecy. *Examples*: 'introverted', 'masks'.

TEXT B

a   Did the mother know her son had not lost the money from the beginning?

b   Which items of vocabulary particularly show the writer's unsympathetic attitude towards the father?

c   Where do you think the family live? What kind of work did the father do?

BOTH TEXTS

Obviously Texts A and B represent very different types of text, but how many similarities can you find in their subject? What kinds of similarity can you find in their subject-matter?

B COMMUNICATIVE ACTIVITIES

1 WHAT GOES WRONG? (see Study Notes, page 121)

Often, when a major accident or fiasco occurs, it is discovered that there is not just one identifiable cause but a list of contributory factors in addition to the main factor.

a   Look at the following examples and, where appropriate, identify them.

b   Discuss what in each case might have been the main or contributory factors in the accident, fiasco etc.

Example: At the end of the Olympic Games the host city discovers that the cost of the games will be approximately nine times as much as was budgeted for. Even after the last athlete had returned home, neither the stadium nor the two Olympic hotels were finished.

POSSIBLE FACTORS

Poor costing of the construction work. Inadequate financial forecasting and control generally. Labour problems? Bad weather? Difficulties with selling TV rights? Overpriced tickets that kept the public away?

i   On her maiden voyage, the world's newest, most magnificent and 'unsinkable' liner travels full steam ahead into a field of icebergs, of which it had been warned by several other ships by radio. As many passengers as possible leave by lifeboat, but 1500 die.

ii   The city decides to commission a foreign architect to build a magnificent new opera house for £5 million. When the beautiful, futuristic building eventually opens – years late – the cost is £55 million and there are no car parks.

iii At a holiday airport on the busiest day of the week and with extra traffic because of diversions, the problem of increasing fog is added to that of traffic congestion. All planes waiting for take-off are experiencing a delay of approximately two hours. A KLM jumbo begins to take off, and at 180 mph smashes into a Pan-Am jumbo on the runway. 582 people die.

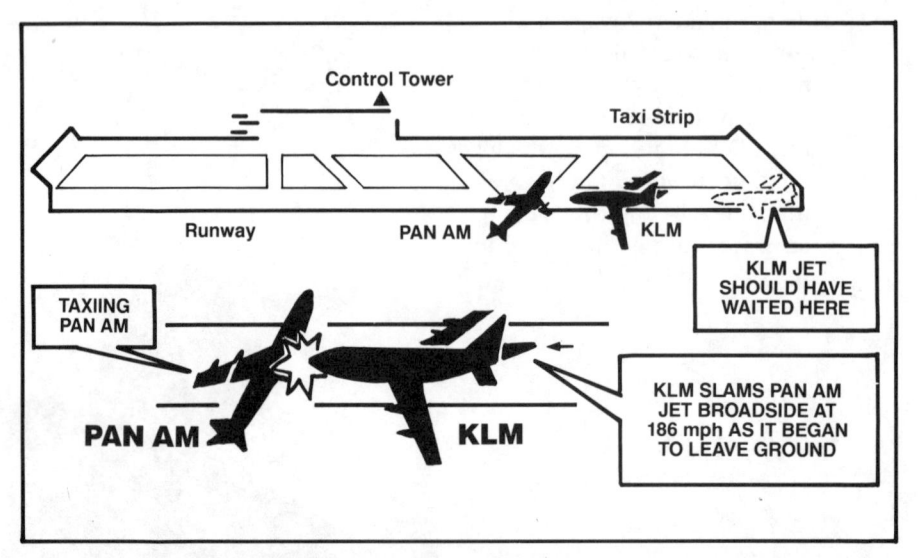

iv Part of a nuclear reactor explodes, causing the deaths either immediately or during the ensuing decade of thousands of people. An inquiry uncovers the fact that safety procedures were regularly ignored.

v Within weeks of its launch, a new daily newspaper in the UK, aimed at providing more serious news coverage, less scandal and fewer 'girlie' pictures, is in financial difficulties and is taken over by a multinational corporation.

ADDUCING CAUSES

2 WHAT MAKES FOR SUCCESS OR CAUSES FAILURE? (see Study Notes, page 121)

Research into why some college students manage to deal with their academic tasks much more successfully than others revealed that the more successful students understand the exact nature of the task, are confident in their approach, know how to marshal facts and arguments, have the determination to follow through their line of argument, and throughout are able to maintain an objectivity that their less successful colleagues find difficult.

a   Study the table in the example and then suggest how you would complete (I)–(III) in a similar way.

Example: University students

Successful	Unsuccessful
Understand instructions	Misunderstand instructions
Approach the problem confidently and decisively	Have a confused approach to the problem
Apply relevant knowledge to the problem	Are unable to apply knowledge they have
Follow through to the conclusion by means of logical steps	Their argument gets lost
Maintain an objective attitude to the problem	Are easily distracted by personal or emotional considerations

I   LECTURERS

Successful

Have a clear and lively delivery.
Their lectures are interesting and have shape.
...
...

Unsuccessful

....
....

Fail to put the students in the picture.
....

II   PARENT OF A 17-YEAR-OLD

Successful

....

Shares some of the child's interests.
Treats the teenager as an individual.
Avoids making judgements about friends, lifestyle, clothes.
....

Unsuccessful

Still sees himself or herself primarily as a parent.
....

....

....

....

TALKING ABOUT SUCCESS AND FAILURE   VERB PATTERNS   FAIL, AVOID, MANAGE.

III NOVELIST
Successful   *Unsuccessful*

Manages to make his characters   ....
seem alive.

....

Is able to think up good plots.   ....

....   Dialogues in books are unnatural.
....   The reader's interest flags.

b   In the same way compare the successful and unsuccessful aspects of other activities of your choice (perhaps your own actual or intended profession).

3   THE OTHER SIDE OF THE COIN (see Study Notes, page 121)

Many positive human qualities have their bad sides: for example, somebody who is very *charming* might also be extremely *vain* and *superficial*. We all know people who are very *lively* and *dynamic* but who are also rather *aggressive* and *domineering* on occasions.

a   Complete the table below with your suggestions as to the negative qualities associated with the positive qualities on the left.

Positive qualities   *Negative qualities*

i   Dynamic, lively, 'the life and   Domineering and manipulative.
     soul of the party'.
ii   Good with money.   Rather ....
iii Marvellous sense of humour, ...
     never stops laughing.
iv   So very tactful and diplomatic.   ....
v   Sociable and gregarious.   ....
vi   He's got that breadth of mind, ...
     he can always see the other side
     of the argument.
vii She's got so much determination   ....
     and strength of character.
viii Very, very sensitive!   ....

b   List what you or your close friends or relatives would say were your best qualities, e.g. determination, easy-goingness.

c   Now consider whether you also have the equivalent 'negative' qualities, e.g. obstinacy, laziness.

4 WAYS OF SAYING 'NO' (see Study Notes, page 122)

There are many different ways of saying 'No' according to the exact context and the degree of strength with which we express ourselves.

Discuss what the negative responses to the following requests might be. Give two or three possibilities, making them increasingly definite.

Example: You want your 13-year-old daughter to change her weekend arrangements. What does she say?

  i   Do I have to?
  ii I'd rather not.
  iii I'm not going to!

a   You ask your bank manager to help you with a further loan to meet unexpected commitments. What does he say?

b   You ask your boss for six months' leave of absence to attend a diploma course. What does he say?

c   You ask someone to marry you, but he or she isn't all that keen! What does he or she say?

d   One of your children asks you to do something you don't want to do. What do you say?

e   An employee asks for permission to write an article for a trade magazine about an engineering process you want to keep very confidential. What do you say to him?

5 MANAGING INTERACTIONS (see Study Notes, page 122)

a   In *Contrasts* (Unit 2) it was observed that one way of looking at everyday expressions such as 'I'm sorry to bother you but . . .', 'I hope I'm not interrupting anything . . .' 'Now you may be wondering why I haven't mentioned . . .' is to say that the speaker is trying to stop the person or persons he or she is speaking to responding negatively or even aggressively.

Discuss how you might disarm people in the following situations and give a complete utterance where possible. Suggest several alternatives if you can.

  i   You'd like to know how much someone paid for her compact disc player, but she's the kind of person who doesn't usually like talking about money matters. What do you say to her?

  ii   You need your secretary to finish a letter urgently, although she already has enough work to last until the end of the working day. How do you ask her?

  iii At a committee meeting you have put a proposal but wish to anticipate the criticism that what you've proposed is really nothing new. What do you say?

  iv   You phone an acquaintance up and they sound rather preoccupied as if they're in the middle of something. What do you say?

RESPONDING NEGATIVELY TO REQUESTS.

v   It's 11.30 p.m. and you have no alternative but to ring up a colleague to ask him what time a meeting is tomorrow morning. He normally goes to bed at 10.30. What do you say to him?

vi   For his own good, you want to advise a colleague to refer a certain matter to the Managing Director. On the other hand, it is, strictly speaking, nothing to do with you. What do you say to your colleague?

vii   You want to advise your 17-year-old daughter against taking up acting as a career, because you don't think she's suited to it. What do you say?

viii   You are giving a talk and wish to tell some members of the audience that you anticipate a certain amount of disagreement from them.

ix   You have been talking for some time but haven't yet got round to the subject of your talk. Anticipate any possible impatience.

x   Anticipate the criticism that you know nothing about the subject you're offering advice on.

B 'PHYSICAL DISARMERS'

Sometimes we employ one or several of the following expressions in order to manage the interaction and disarm the other person: a low 'intimate' tone of voice, smiles, winks, eye-contact, certain facial expressions, touch.

Consider which of the above might be used to win the other person over in the following cases:

i   Making 'difficult' requests (e.g. (ii) above).

ii   When you've done something wrong or made a mistake and somebody in authority brings it to your notice. (You'e parked your car illegally, and when you return to it you find a traffic warden or policeman just about to book (or fine) you.)

ROLE PLAY

Two students act out (i) and (ii) using their chosen 'physical disarmers'.

6 LANGUAGE GAMES
A DON'T SAY 'YES' OR 'NO'

The teacher or chairperson asks individuals rapid questions, such as:

It's Tuesday today, isn't it?
You're Barbara, aren't you?
You live in X, don't you?
Are you sitting next to Tom?

and the students must answer *immediately* but *without* using the words 'yes' or 'no'. Here are some useful answers:

Not yet/I think so/Certainly not/Indeed it is/That is my name/That's correct/Not as far as I know/I do indeed/Quite correct/Not at the moment.

If a team answers too slowly, it loses a turn. The team which manages to answer most questions without making a 'mistake' wins.

B ALL WRONG

Can you correct all the mistakes in this 'ungrammatical poem'?

What a wonderful bird the frog are.
When he sit, he stand almost;
When he leap, he fly almost
He ain't got no sense hardly;
He ain't got no tail hardly either.
When he sit, he sit on what he ain't got – almost.

C LISTENING ACTIVITIES

It can be very difficult to identify when people are really saying 'No'. For a variety of reasons we use different methods to refuse to comply. A child who is told to go to sleep may deliberately keep himself awake. A patient who is told to take certain tablets may neglect to do so. A secretary who is suddenly ordered to make 14 cups of tea may respond by producing a completely undrinkable beverage. A student who finds his essay covered in meaningless comments written in red ink may decide not to make any further effort.

1 a Working in groups of three or four, share your experiences of ways of saying no. You may be able to relate to the examples you have been given.
      Appoint a scribe who will be responsible for noting down all relevant points and reporting back to the entire group of students.

   b Now discuss why the child, the patient, the secretary and the student might have refused to comply. The scribe should report your conclusions.

2 Psychologists have defined four general areas of behavioural patterns in an attempt refuse. These are: being assertive; aggressive; submissive; manipulative. Look at the interaction chart in Unit 5 on page 76 and discuss in your group whether the responses are in category i, ii, iii or iv.

3 a Listen to the taped interactions.
   b Use the interaction chart and your example as a guide.
   c Discuss your reactions with other members of your group.

D STRUCTURE AND LANGUAGE USAGE

1 DID IT HAPPEN OR NOT? (see Study Notes, page 122)

With some verb forms it is often quite difficult for non-native speakers to decide whether or not the event referred to actually happened.

In pairs look at the following sentences and then discuss the answer to the questions in brackets.

a   We were going to Portugal last year. (Did they actually go?)

b   I wish we'd taken our cameras. (Did they take their cameras?)

c   Even though they went they didn't see much. (But did they go in fact?)

d   It would have been better if we'd left at that point. (Did they leave at that point?)

e   He needn't have provided so much food. (Was the food provided by him or not?)

f   I'd rather Jane went. (Has Jane already gone?)

g   I'd rather Tom had gone. (Did Tom go?)

h   This was to have been the culmination of the year. (Was it in fact?)

i   We were to have gone to London today. (Did they go?)

j   Had they known, they would have come. (Did they know?)

2 BUT HE DIDN'T . . . (see Study Notes, page 122)

discard	reject	repeal	back out	suppress	cancel	quash	rescind
break off	turn down	give up	stop	deny	withdraw	sever	decline
refuse							

Check that you know the vocabulary both in the box and in the examples below. Then complete the following with one of the verbs in the box.

Example: They invited us a couple of weeks ago but we *declined*. (or *turned it down*)

a   We all begged him to do it, but he ....

b   Mark used to smoke 40 cigarettes a day, but now ....

c   Tom applied for the job, but ....

d   The twins play with a new toy for about two days and then ....

e   They arranged a further meeting, but two days later they ....

f   At first permission was officially given, but then it was ....

g   The Act was passed during the last few weeks of the Labour Government, but the incoming Conservative Government ....

h   He made a visa application, but it ....

i   The couple were sentenced to five years, but on appeal the sentence ....

j   At first he admitted taking part in the crime, but now ....

k   At one time a number of opposition parties were permitted, but in recent years ....

l   As a result of the rift, all diplomatic ties have been ....

m   Everything was fine until the planning inquiry, when the plans were ....

n   They had promised to come round and help us move, but ....

3 DIFFICULT NEGATIVES

Make these sentences negative. (*Warning*: there are special difficulties involved.)

a   We think so too.
b   I think it's a pretty good idea.
c   You'd better go to the doctor's.
d   Someone open the door!
e   We expect her to win easily.
f   They've got enough supplies already.
g   This has been the case for a very long time.
h   We've still got a long way to go.
i   I'd rather work in London if I have the choice.
j   This already applies to some of the people working here.
k   I suppose someone knows the answer.
l   The car should be ready by now.

E WRITING ACTIVITIES

1 Look at Section B2.
   Make your own analysis of successful and unsuccessful approaches to an area of life you have experience or knowledge of but did not deal with in class. Write out the analysis in the form of a connected passage.

2 EXTENSION

An elderly actor writes a short article in a popular monthly magazine with a predominantly young readership (16–30), warning against the dangers of being lured by the bright lights of the theatre. Read the text carefully and then do the writing activity suggested.

A warning to all aspiring actors and actresses
To anyone who tells me they want to go on the stage I say 'Have you gone mad? Are you sufficiently out of your mind?' I try to discourage him or her with stories of young actors or actresses who have yielded to the glamour of the stage only to have their hopes disappointed, their personal finances ruined and their chances of a successful career in another profession seriously impaired, if not destroyed.

You are still interested? Well, have you thought of what it's really like to have to discipline and repress your own personality almost to the point of extinction simply to represent a character, perhaps a minor one, in an imperfect production to a half-empty hall in a matinée? Most important of all, have you thought of the consequences for what we consider normal family life – the exhausting tours far from home, staying in third-rate boarding houses, coming home emotionally and physically drained at 11.30 pm six nights a week?

Still interested? Welcome to the madhouse!

Now write a similar article warning young people of the difficulties they might expect to encounter if they attempt one of the following:

a go into politics

b give up their career to become a full-time parent

c try to become a top racing driver

d a career of your choice

STUDY NOTES

A1 READING

Text B

'A ten-shilling note' and 'a sixpence': these were dropped when Britain adopted decimal currency. They were equivalent to 50p and $2\frac{1}{2}$p.

B1 WHAT GOES WRONG?

Useful vocabulary for discussion

i   overconfidence; to be overconfident; the latest shipbuilding technology; lifeboats; to man a radio; to pass on warnings; radar

ii   to cost a design; to estimate the cost of something; to predict; to foresee; architectural plans; contractors; labour; politicians; personality clashes; design faults

iii   to divert a plane (e.g. because of bad weather at another airport); stress; overwork; visibility; impatience; confusion

iv   supervision; to supervise; to observe safety precautions; foolproof systems; reactor-design; chain of command; inadequate; insufficient; negligence

v   to overestimate; to underestimate; circulation; competition; to undercapitalise; financial backing; market-research; new technology

B2 WHAT MAKES FOR SUCCESS OR CAUSES FAILURE?

Useful vocabulary for discussion

i   monotonous; to mumble; unclear diction; shapeless; to have structure; to wander from the point; to digress; to ramble; background information; handouts; give an overview of the subject; relate to the rest of the subject

ii   to share interests, hobbies etc.; to take an interest in; to respect somebody's individuality; to make judgements; to be critical of; to talk down to

iii   unreal; unrealistic; contrived; a 'shaky' plot; to hold/keep up someone's interest; to maintain the suspense; style; to make people keep reading; to feel you know the characters

B3 THE OTHER SIDE OF THE COIN

Useful vocabulary for discussion (not in order of the questions)

mean; careful; flippant; superficial; moody; manipulative; domineering; indecisive; secretive; vulnerable; wilful; obstinate; stubborn; ineffectual

B4 WAYS OF SAYING 'NO'

Useful vocabulary for discussion (not in order of the questions)

Study the following and decide which are appropriate to which of the situations:
I'm afraid it's out of the question; Of course we'd like to . . .; Obviously I'd prefer to be able to say 'yes' . . .; I'll see darling; We'd much rather you didn't; I'd rather not; I'm just not in a position to . . .; the answer's 'no', I'm very sorry . . .; it's not on Jim, sorry (colloquial); I must ask you not to go ahead; The answer's going to have to be 'no'; Look Jim/I'm very fond of you/you're very sweet/you're very sweet to ask, but . . .

B5 MANAGING INTERACTIONS

Useful vocabulary for discussion (not in order of the questions)

Study the following and consider which are appropriate to each situation:
Look, you know I wouldn't interfere, but . . .; Hope I haven't interrupted anything . . .; It's none of my business, but . . .; You will be wondering when I will get to my subject; Not all of you will agree with this . . .; Now, you might say this is nothing new, but . . .; I know you're very busy, but do you think you could possibly . . .; Some of you may well disagree with this, but . . .; Whilst not pretending to be an expert on . . ./to know a great deal about . . .; I hope you don't mind my asking, but . . .

D1 DID IT HAPPEN OR NOT?

Study the following examples and then use the information they provide on structures when completing the exercises on page 118.

There were lots of empty seats; *we needn't have booked.*
Jim behaved so badly, *it would have been better* if he hadn't come.
I was going to do some decorating, but a couple of friends called round.
Shall I go on my own? No, *I'd rather we both went.*
I wish I'd brought the umbrella. Never mind we can stay inside.
Tragic about George – *he was to have retired next May.* When's the funeral?
Been here long? About an hour? *Had I realised* I'd have come earlier.

D2 BUT HE DIDN'T . . .

Study the following newspaper headlines and use the information they provide on meaning and usage when you complete D2 (N.B. They do not give examples of *all* the vocabulary)

PARLIAMENT SET TO REPEAL SUNDAY CLOSING LAWS

BRITAIN SEVERS LINKS WITH LIBYA

7
STUDY NOTES

BANK BACKS OUT OF LOAN CONSORTIUM

DISCARDED PAINTING WAS REMBRANDT

LOCAL COMPANY TURNED DOWN FOR U.S. CONTRACT

£10,000 FINE QUASHED ON APPEAL

MINISTER DENIES KNOWLEDGE OF LEAK

7
STUDY NOTES

8 EMPHASIS
Giving prominence to certain information; talking about priorities

A READING TEXTS

1 READING

See Unit 1, Section A (page 5) for instructions. Text B for this unit will be found on page 181.

Text A

WAYS OF SEEING by John Berger

What distinguishes oil painting from any other form of painting is its special ability to render the tangibility, the texture, the lustre, the solidity of what it depicts. It defines the real as that which you can put your hands on.

Although its painted images are two-dimensional, its potential of illusionism is far greater than that of sculpture, for it can suggest objects possessing colour, texture and temperature, filling a space and, by implication, filling the entire world.

Holbein's painting of 'The Ambassadors' (1533) stands at the beginning of the tradition and, as often happens with a work at the opening of a new period, its character is undisguised. The way it is painted shows what it is about. How is it painted?

It is painted with great skill to create the illusion in the spectator that he is looking at real objects and materials. We pointed out in the first essay that the sense of touch was like a restricted, static sense of sight. Every square inch of the surface of this painting, whilst remaining purely visual, appeals to, importunes, the sense of touch. The eye moves from fur to silk to metal to wood to velvet to marble to paper to felt, and each time what the eye perceives is already translated, within the painting itself, into the language of tactile sensation. The two men have a certain presence and there are many objects which symbolise ideas, but it is the materials, the stuff, by which the men are surrounded and clothed which dominate the painting.

Except for the faces and hands, there is not a surface in this picture which does not make one aware of how it has been elaborately worked over – by weavers, embroiderers, carpet-makers, goldsmiths, leather workers, mosaic-makers, furriers, tailors, jewellers – and of how this working-over and the resulting richness of each surface has been finally worked-over and reproduced by Holbein the painter.

'The Ambassadors' by Hans Holbein the Younger, reproduced by courtesy of the Trustees, National Gallery, London

This emphasis and the skill that lay behind it was to remain a constant of the tradition of oil painting.

Works of art in earlier traditions celebrated wealth. But wealth was then a symbol of a fixed social or divine order. Oil painting celebrated a new kind of wealth – which was dynamic and which found its only sanction in the supreme buying power of money. Thus painting itself had to be able to demonstrate the desirability of what money could buy. And the visual desirability of what can be bought lies in its tangibility, in how it will reward the touch, the hand, of the owner.

Until very recently – and in certain milieux even today – a certain moral value was ascribed to the study of the classics. This was because the classic texts, whatever their intrinsic worth, supplied the higher strata of the ruling class with a system of references for the forms of their own idealised behaviour. As well as poetry, logic and philosophy, the classics offered a system of etiquette. They offered examples of how the heightened moments of life – to be found in heroic action, the dignified exercise of power, passion, courageous death, the noble pursuit of pleasure – should be lived, or, at least, should be seen to be lived.

Yet why are these pictures so vacuous and so perfunctory in their evocation of the scenes they are meant to recreate? They did not need to stimulate the imagination. If they had, they would have served their purpose less well. Their purpose was not to transport their spectator-owners into new experience, but to embellish such experience as they already possessed. Before these canvases the spectator-owner hoped to see the classic face of his own passion or grief or generosity. The idealised appearances he found in the painting were an aid, a support, to his own view of himself. In those appearances he found the guise of his own (or his wife's or his daughters') nobility.

John Berger, *Ways of Seeing*, BBC and Penguin, 1972

2 QUESTIONS ON THE TEXTS

TEXT A

a What is the ideological emphasis of John Berger's article?

b To what extent can you sympathise with his argument?

TEXT B

a What aspect(s) of the behaviour of football fans is Peter Marsh emphasising and how does this contrast with the general view of football hooliganism?

b 'A lot of fashionable sociologists romanticise problems such as violence or crime and are themselves part of the problem.' Do you agree?

BOTH TEXTS

'Both texts result from intellectuals over-analysing areas of life that do not really lend themselves to such analysis.' What do you think?

B COMMUNICATIVE ACTIVITIES

1 TALKING ABOUT IMPRESSIONS (see Study Notes, page 136)

a Psychologists tell us that when we meet somebody for the first time we decide whether or not we like them in the first four minutes and that we only very rarely change our minds about them afterwards. We are particularly influenced by physical appearance, body language, manners, speech, and attitudes.

  i Make lists of the things (not only physical) you notice about people on first meeting them, and then compare them with the lists compiled by other members of the group.

ii   It often happens that our first contact with somebody does not involve actually meeting them in person, but is by letter or phone, in which case other factors may come into play to create our first impression of them. Discuss which different factors would contribute to your impression of somebody if you were limited to the following types of contact:

By phone	By letter, memo etc.	Other people's conversation	Seen on TV
....	Quality of paper?	....	....
....	....	....	....

iii Are there situations in which you make a special effort to influence or impress people, for example by your dress, physical appearance, or the way you speak to and treat people? How do you approach this task of impression-management?

iv   What are the things that you think people notice about you? Consult the group. Do people sometimes get the wrong idea about you?

v   Is there generally a disparity between what we should be looking for in the people we meet and what we are in fact impressed by?

B INTERVIEWS (see Study Notes, page 136)

To most people, going for an interview, whether for an educational place or a new job, is categorised as one of life's least pleasant experiences. What makes it unpleasant is the knowledge that you only have a certain very limited time in which to make a favourable impression on the interviewing panel and that they, unless you manage to emphasise your strong points and play down your weak points, might never know how very suitable you were!

What are interviewers looking for? Someone with long experience of selection panels said they paid particular attention to the following:

i   The way the interviewee answers the questions put to him or her.

ii   The applicant's physical appearance, personality and interactional skills.

iii The attitude of the applicant to the panel of interviewers.

iv   How willingly an applicant enlarges upon a subject.

1   Go through (i)–(iv) above and discuss what exactly is meant by each item, referring where possible to your own experience of interviews. Is the list complete, in your view?

2   What do you try to emphasise about yourself when you go for an interview? (Relate your points to (i)–(iv) above.)

3   Give typical examples of what might happen under (i)–(iv) in an interview which was a disaster. For example being very hesitant might come under (i). Once again refer where possible to your own experience.

👥 2 IT MUST BE EMPHASISED THAT ... (see Study Notes, page 136)

At the time of the 1986 nuclear power station accident at Chernobyl, in the USSR, British government ministers appearing on TV and radio were questioned about the danger to UK food supplies, especially milk, meat and vegetables, from nuclear fallout. During these interviews the officials concerned repeatedly emphasised the following points in order to prevent any panic reactions by the public:

That government scientists were closely monitoring the situation.

That radiation levels were well within existing safety limits and that therefore there was no cause for alarm.

That there was absolutely no need for housewives to change their shopping habits.

a Look at the following situations and discuss which points the people concerned would probably wish to emphasise in order to allay people's fears or prevent an already difficult situation from further deteriorating.

b Discuss what actual language they might use to emphasise those points.

   i   The US President has just come out of hospital after a surprise two-day stay for preventative surgery. The White House Press Officer calls a press conference to counter rumours that the President is suffering from terminal cancer.

   ii   The workforce are concerned at media reports confirming the takeover of their firm by a foreign transnational company with a reputation for buying out and then closing down smaller companies simply in order to eliminate competition. The Managing Director calls a meeting, attended by a representative of the new parent company, to reassure them.

   iii Several seriously contaminated cartons of baby food have been discovered by public health officials. The Press Officer of the company seeks to reassure the public and limit the damage to the company's name.

   iv   A microcomputer firm has got into financial difficulties because of a fall-off in orders in the run-up to Christmas, and crucial secret talks with their financial advisers, their own bank and a merchant bank are taking place with a view to raising cash to save the company. But then the business reporter of the local newspaper rings up and says he's heard rumours that the company is in difficulty. It is decided that you, as the Press Officer, should admit to some very temporary cash-flow problems while emphasising other positive developments.

   v   A sixteen-year-old girl has run away from home and not been in contact with her family for three days. She's been staying at a girlfriend's house and isn't in any trouble. She now phones her mother for the first time.

GIVING PROMINENCE TO CERTAIN INFORMATION

3 PROVERBS, SAYINGS AND QUOTATIONS (see Study Notes, page 136)

a   All the following sayings, proverbs, or quotations emphasise one thing at the expense of others. After working on the Study Notes and finding out what they mean, express the meanings of the proverbs in as many ways as possible.

  i   Money talks.
  ii   It's not what you know, it's who you know.
  iii   He who knows how to be poor, knows everything. (Jules Michelet)
  iv   Choose a wife rather by your ear than your eye. (Thomas Fuller)
  v   It's no good crying over spilt milk.
  vi   A bird in the hand is worth two in the bush.
  vii   Life is what happens to us while we're making plans. (John Lennon)
  viii Manners makyth Man. (the motto of Winchester College, England's oldest public school)
  ix   Don't count your chickens before they're hatched.
  x   The proof of the pudding is in the eating.

b   Which do you think are particularly (i) true? (ii) untrue?

EXPRESSING EMPHASIS

4 HAVE THEY GOT THEIR PRIORITIES RIGHT?

All the following newspaper items stress the overriding importance of certain qualities or qualifications. Read them carefully and then consider how you would answer the questions below:

i   Flat-lettings in SW1. Privately-educated tenants only may apply.

ii   In Kyoto five members of a top karate club are arrested for kicking a fellow-member to death for wearing a dirty karate suit.

iii   FEMININE lady, attractive, warm personality, varied interests, seeks presentable, tall, educated man, house and car owner, aged 55 to 65, for lasting sincere relationship.

iv   MALE 29, London NW3. Wishes to meet female interested in studying with me for Solicitor's Clerk exams. Write to Kevin, Box 29710.

v   City of London. Oxbridge applicants sought for positions as financial trainees.

vi   ENGLISH TEACHERS required for London. Experience/qualifications not essential. Smart appearance, personality and accent more important.

vii   Architect, 50s, divorced. Manchester. Seeks professional woman with boarding-school education. Must be under 50, interested in sport, and certainly not overweight, preferably size 12–14.

viii

Women's Events

Women's Videos
Sat July 12th, 2–6pm

Women only, 20p admission, free creche
Women's Resources Centre,

The Fabulous Dirt Sisters

Women's band on Friday July 18th, 7.30pm
At Alton Community Centre
Women only. Tickets £3 and £2 unwaged

Tickets can only be bought in advance

a   Is it justifiable that advertisements (i) and (v) should be allowed to stipulate certain candidates?

b   Are the advertisers in (iii), (vii) and (viii) being foolish or sensible in setting so many conditions? Is it prejudice or just that they know what they want?

c   What do you think about (iv)? If you were a woman reading the advertisement, what would you think about Kevin? Would you like being called a female?

d   Look at (ii) and (vi). Have they got their priorities right?

C LISTENING ACTIVITIES

1. Listen to this discussion and try to determine:
   a. the relationship of the speakers
   b. the topic
   c. the priorities of each of the three speakers
   d. the significance of certain stressed words and how this stress emphasises the attitude of the speaker
      i. *Do* be quiet, Helen.
      ii. Sense? *I'll* give you sense.
      iii. Not for *me* it isn't.
      iv. Now I can make up my *own* mind.
      v. I *certainly* do.

   When you have drawn some conclusions, compare these with two or three other members of the class.

2. You are about to hear the sort of interview that may take place almost every day of the year. The applicant is 19 and there are three members of the interviewing panel. Listen very carefully to:
   a. the type and form of questions
   b. the reaction of the interviewee to different questions
   c. what seems to be the emphasis of the individual panel members

   When you have formed some ideas, go on to discuss how suitable and relevant you found the questions and answers to be and how you would have felt and behaved had you been the interviewee. For example, would you have felt that the panel were interested in you? Did any of the panel members follow up their questions?

PART 3

   a. The interviewing panel are discussing the future prospects of Henry, the candidate. Listen to their conversation and discuss:
      i. the different reactions of the panel members to Henry.
      ii. why the reactions are different.
   b. Then work with some of your group to finish the conversation. You will need to make lists of priorities, for example:

For	**Against**
Lives locally	Wants accommodation here
Seems committed	Too keen

D STRUCTURE AND LANGUAGE USAGE

1 THE LANGUAGE OF EMPHASIS (see Study Notes, page 136)

Make new sentences of approximately the same meaning, using the items given below each sentence:

a The professor was very emphatic about not wanting to attend the seminar.
   i emphasise   ii stress (verb)

b My school emphasised the importance of team-sports and self-reliance.
   i put/stress   ii a lot of emphasis ...

c Islam lays great stress on the importance of the family.
   i The importance ...   ii crucially important
   iii crucial importance

d His inexperience in this field was made more obvious by the presence of so many experts at the meeting.
   i accentuate   ii point up   iii What made ...

e The new campaign will emphasise fitness and health.
   i accent (noun)   ii great stress

f The totally empty background points up the lively activity in the foreground. (talking about a painting)
   i prominence   ii prominent   iii emphasis

2 (see Study Notes, page 137)

Here are some examples of the ways we employ to give emphasis to what we say. Look at the first example and then discuss how to make other emphatic versions for (b)–(g). Of course it will not always be possible to use exactly the same structures and sometimes there are only two or three possibilities.

Example:

	Emphatic
They serve very good food here.	Very good food they serve here!
	Really excellent food they serve here!
	What excellent food they serve here!
	The food they serve here is so good!
	The food here is amazingly good!

a The Pearsons are friendly people.
b Brighton is a nice place to live.
c *The Name of the Rose* is an interesting book.

EXPRESSING EMPHASIS   'WHAT' IN EXCLAMATORY SENTENCES

d   You've made a very good point.
e   The sequence of famine, starvation and death must not happen again.
f   I don't doubt what you say for a moment.
g   We will only beat unemployment by investing in jobs.

3   BUT OF COURSE . . .

Discuss how to respond positively to the following offers, invitations, suggestions and enquiries in three *increasingly emphatic ways*.

Example: Do you like Indian cooking?
Yes, I do!
Yes, indeed!
I absolutely love it!

a   Like a coffee?
b   How about coming with us?
c   Do you remember me?
d   Did you like Mexico?
e   You like horror-films don't you?
f   Have some more sweet?
g   OK if I come along too?
h   Shall we go to the theatre?
i   Cigarette?
j   Like a lift?

4   USING MORE COLOURFUL LANGUAGE (see Study Notes page 137)

We often respond to a question by choosing a different, stronger adjective or expression e.g. Were you hungry? 'I was absolutely *starving*!'
   Look at the following exchanges and suggest several ways of completing them in a similar way to the example.

Example: Did you like it? We loved every moment! We thought it was marvellous! It was out of this world!

a   Were they cross?

b   Interesting lecture?

c   Does he like her?

d   Is she good looking?

e   Tired?

f   Was it bad?

g   Good food?

h   Did you have to wait long?

i   Was it funny?

USING MORE EXPRESSIVE LANGUAGE

E WRITING ACTIVITIES

1   Write a more emphatic version of the sentences below. Begin the new sentences with the words given:

Example:
(Said at a meeting) I'm saying it's a difficult thing to co-ordinate.
What I'm saying is that it's a difficult thing to co-ordinate.

a   The only way to find out what it's really like is to go there yourself.
    i   Only   ii   It's ....
b   You should only ring that number in an absolute emergency.
    i   Only .... number.   ii   Only .... rung.
c   Nobody should touch those controls under any circumstances.
    i   Under   ii   Those controls ....
d   You forgot to mention that this would be your last visit here.
    What ....
e   They have only very recently begun to appreciate the possible consequences.
    i   Only   ii   It ....
f   We eventually came to an agreement after weeks of negotiation.
    i   It   ii   Only ....
g   The whole platoon was killed. Not ....
h   (At a meeting) I'm trying to say I think it's feasible.
    What ....
i   (At a meeting) He's making the point that these arrangements can't be sorted out overnight. The point ....

2 EXTENSION: TEXT IMPROVEMENT

almost everybody	dread (verb)	intensely	close (adj.)
the great majority	hate	particularly	the closest
every (last) detail of	even though	utterly	total (adj.)
a lottery	still	completely	complete (adj.)
a gamble	only	totally	naked
have a crucial influence	merely	crucially	
from start to finish		openly	
from the very beginning		freely	
at the mercy of			
despite the fact that			
have a dread of			

8

INVERSION

The following text on the subject of interviews uses language that is rather flat. Read it through and think about possible ways of achieving greater emphasis at the points marked with numbers. To help you there are suggestions as to the kind of change you could make below the text and some of the language items you may wish to use are given in the box at the bottom of the opposite page. (Do not feel you have to use the language in the box.) When you are ready, write out an improved version of the text.

    (1)   (2)   (3)
Most people dislike interviews: The experience of having your personality,
                 (4)   (5)   (6)
knowledge and career under scrutiny is an unnerving one. They feel vulnerable
                       (7)   (8)
and know they are taking part in a competition the result of which will influence
(9)   (10)   (11)
their lives. A careless word or facial expression might make the difference
                      (12)
between success and failure and it is depressing to the unsuccessful candidate to
        (13)   (14)   (15)
know that although everybody admits that an interview is often a matter of luck
   (16)   (17)
they will take the result seriously and apportion blame or admiration accordingly.
(18)   (19)
It is painful to learn after an unsuccessful interview, as you walk away from the
                                   (20)
scene of the battle promising yourself that you will never submit to such
                        (21)
indignities again, that the winner was a compromise candidate or that it was all an
    (22)
inside job.

NOTES

(1) Can you make it stronger? (2) Can you make it stronger at this point? Either keep 'dislike' and add an adverb or use a stronger verb on its own. Alternatively you could use a verbal phrase. (3) Can you strengthen it by adding a phrase? (4) An adjective? (5) An adverb? (6) An adverb, phrase or stronger adjective? (7) Emphasise the aspect of chance? (8) An adverb or phrase? (9) Strengthen using 'rest', or 'whole' and 'rest'? (10) A small change in the article and 'just' to give emphasis? (11) Can you add one small word after 'make'? (12) Give emphasis by replacing 'it is' with 'what is particularly . . .' (see Study Notes to B3, page 136). (13) Can you replace with something slightly stronger? (14) An adverb? (15) An adverb? (16) Add a word from the box after 'will' to strengthen. (17) An adverb? (18) Begin with 'what'? (19) A different verb suggestive of pain or injury? (20) You could achieve greater emphasis by using 'inversion' (see D2, page 137). (21) An adverb? (22) Strengthen with a phrase?

8

STUDY NOTES

B1 TALKING ABOUT IMPRESSIONS

Useful vocabulary for discussion

a   The way she sits/stands/talks; whether or not he smiles/looks into your eyes; eye contact; tone of voice; to be a good listener; to make a good impression (3); to make them think I'm . . . (3); physical factors (5); human qualities (5); character (5);

b Interviews: useful vocabulary for discussion

(i) hesitation, to hesitate; quick to answer; to know your subject; to be confident/diffident; an ability to 'field' questions (To field means to deal with a question by answering it or avoiding answering it or even asking another question before you answer it. Politicians 'field' questions, ordinary people answer them!); to interact well . . ./to be good with people . . ./to know how to get on with people; (iii) to charm people; to inspire confidence; (iv) to elaborate/enlarge on a subject; to go into detail about; hostile questions; to waffle (talk very vaguely and at length); to seem tongue-tied

B2 IT MUST BE EMPHASISED THAT . . .

Useful vocabulary for discussion

It should be emphasised/stressed that; There is absolutely no cause for (public) anxiety; There are no plans to . . .; Rumours that . . . are completely without foundation/groundless; We wish to emphasise that . . .; an isolated incident (iii); a very temporary cash-flow problem; absolutely no need to worry (v); Really, there's no problem (v); You really mustn't/don't have to worry (v); Everything's all right (v); Nothing's wrong, absolutely nothing (v).

B3 PROVERBS, SAYINGS AND QUOTATIONS

Useful vocabulary for discussion

What's important is . . .; The important/crucial thing is . . .; What really matters is . . .; it's money that really matters; You might think the important thing is . . . but in fact . . .

D1 THE LANGUAGE OF EMPHASIS

a   Study the following sentences and then use the information on structures they provide to complete D1 on page 132.

The government *emphasises/stresses* that it wants to modify the bill before it comes to Parliament; Generally speaking, Protestantism *puts a lot of stress/emphasis* on individual responsibility; At the interview a *lot of emphasis/stress was put on* the need to be a self-starter; The importance of increased investment *was stressed/emphasised* at the monthly board meeting; Positive attitudes are *crucially important/of crucial importance* at interviews; The plight of the refugees was *accentuated by* their lack of adequate clothing; *What made* Marxism so attractive to these people was the rational explanation it offered for their economic position; First reports suggest that at this year's Paris fashion shows, the *accent* will be on textures; The Roman Catholic Church gives a much greater degree of *prominence* to the Virgin Mary than the Protestant Church.

D2 INSTRUCTIONS ARE AS FOR D1 ABOVE.

What a nice car that is!
- **e** You've done an unusually good job.
- **f** Never again will I go to that restaurant!
- **g** Not for a million pounds will I marry that man!; I certainly don't disbelieve what you say; I don't in any way question what you've told us but . . .
- **h** It was only by paying £25 for a taxi that we managed to catch the train; Knocking on doors is the only way to get the opportunities you want; The only way you can succeed in that business is by getting to know the right people!

D4 USING MORE COLOURFUL LANGUAGE

Useful language for completing the exercise

absolutely furious; livid; dreadful; unbelievably awful; (absolutely) fascinating; (so) delicious; crazy about her; totally in love with; infatuated with; for absolute ages; for hours; for hours and hours; for hours on end; (absolutely) shattered
(colloquial / exhausted / finished; stunningly beautiful; hilarious; we couldn't stop laughing

8
STUDY NOTES

9 IN THE MIND

Academic subjects, mental qualities, activities, attitudes and associations

A READING TEXTS

1 READING

See Unit 1, Section A (page 5) for instructions. Text B for this unit will be found on page 182.

Text A

'AN ESSAY ON SCIANS' by Sir Peter Medawar

That which in the English-speaking world is known by everyone as 'science' was not always so designated. The *Oxford English Dictionary* proffers the following homophones: sienz, ciens, cience, siens, syence, syense, scyence, scyense, scyens, scienc, sciens, scians. Of these, I like best the one I have chosen, though I am sad that the others are out of work. All derive, of course, from 'scientia', knowledge, but no one construes 'science' merely as knowledge. It is thought of rather as knowledge hard won, in which we have much more confidence than we have in opinion, hearsay and belief. The word 'science' itself is used as a general name for, on the one hand, the procedures of science-adventures of thought and stratagems of inquiry that go into the advancement of learning – and on the other hand, the substantive body of knowledge that is the outcome of this complex endeavour, though this latter is no mere pile of information: Science is organised knowledge, everyone agrees, and this organisation goes much deeper than the pedagogic subdivision into the conventional '-ologies', each pigeon-holed into lesser topics. Science is, or aspires to be, deductively ordered: It parades principles, laws and other general statements from which statements about ordinary particulars follow as theorems. The sciences don't begin this way, to be sure; nor do they always end in this tidy, deductively ordered form. Samuel Taylor Coleridge, writing *A Preliminary Treatise on Method*, complained that zoology as he studied it was so weighed down and crushed by a profusion of particular information, 'without evincing the least promise of systematising itself by any inward combination of its parts', that it was in danger of falling apart. It was of course Linnaeus and Darwin and those whom they inspired who rescued zoology from the odium of being no more than a heap of ostensibly unrelated facts. All the sciences that we judge mature have the kind of internal connectedness which Coleridge deplored the absence of in zoology. This kind of connectedness, or holding-togetherness, gives the sciences great stability and power to assimilate more information: In a long-established science it is impossible to imagine a situation in which a single phenomenon could so shake its foundations that it might all come tumbling down. Correspondingly, science is never long in a turmoil of self-questioning about its fundamental premises and assumptions. Another property that sets the genuine sciences apart from those that arrogate to themselves the title without really earning it is their predictive capability: Newton and cosmology generally are tested by every entry in a nautical almanac and corroborated every time the tide rises or recedes according to the book, as it is also corroborated by the periodic reappearance on schedule of, for example, Halley's comet (next due, 1986). I expect that its embarrassing infirmity of prediction has been the most important single factor that denies the coveted designation 'science' to, for example, economics.

Peter Medawar, *The Limits of Science*, Oxford University Press, 1986

2 QUESTIONS ON THE TEXTS

TEXT A

a   Which of the following academic subjects would be allowed as sciences according to Sir Peter Medawar's definition? Physics, psychology, geology, sociology, linguistics, astronomy, mathematics.

b   Do you agree with his definition, or should it be broader in your opinion?

TEXT B

a   Does Walter Mitty exist only in literature or is there a Walter Mitty inside most of us?

b   Do you regard such daydreams and imaginings as a danger to or an embellishment of day-to-day life?

B COMMUNICATIVE ACTIVITIES

1 ACADEMIC DISCIPLINES (see Study Notes, page 149)

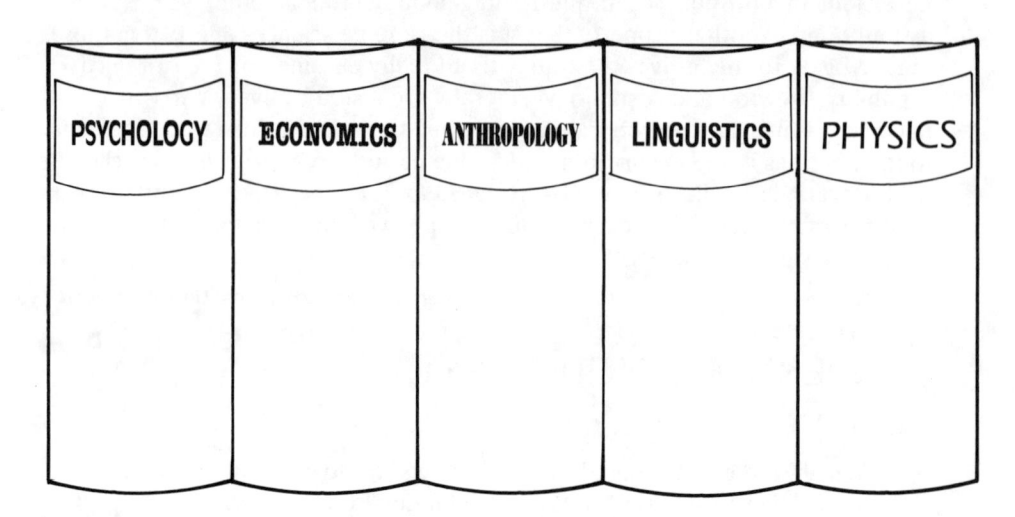

[Illustration of five books standing upright, labelled: PSYCHOLOGY, ECONOMICS, ANTHROPOLOGY, LINGUISTICS, PHYSICS]

Example:
Chemistry – the science that deals with the composition, structure and properties of substances and the transformations that they undergo.

a   In pairs, choose one of the five subjects in the above illustration (or one of your own choice if you prefer) and give a *general* account of what it involves. An example has been done for you. Bear in mind the following questions:

   i   What does this discipline study?
   ii   What does this discipline seek to explain?
   iii How do the data or insights it provides benefit other fields of study and society in general?

b   Which, in your opinion, are the more truly scientific subjects?

c   Sociolinguistics, psycholinguistics, semantics and phonology are all branches of linguistics, with their own fields of interest, research methods and history. Choose an academic subject and say which branches it divides into, pointing out how they differ from each other in aims, procedure, and in their actual or potential benefit to the rest of society.

d   Give the rest of the group an idea of the recent developments in the subject you talked about in (a) above.

e   Talk to the rest of the group about which qualities of mind and personality create an aptitude for this subject.

CONTRASTING FIELDS OF STUDY

2 ATTITUDES AND QUALITIES OF MIND (see Study Notes, page 150)

a   The First World War (1914–18) was a particularly tragic war, with terrible casualties on both sides. (During the Battle of the Somme, for instance, the British suffered 600,000 casualties and the Germans 650,000.)

   i   Read the following poem and discuss the mental attitudes it displays.

The Soldier

If I should die, think only this of me:
That there's some corner of a foreign field
That is for ever England. There shall be
In that rich earth a richer dust concealed;
A dust whom England bore, shaped, made aware,
Gave once, her flowers to love, her ways to roam,
A body of England's, breathing English air,
Washed by the rivers, blest by suns of home.

And think, this heart, all evil shed away,
A pulse in the eternal mind, no less
Gives somewhere back the thoughts by England given;
Her sights and sounds; dreams happy as her day;
And laughter, learnt of friends; and gentleness.
In hearts at peace, under an English heaven.

Rupert Brooke

DISCUSSING ATTITUDES OF MIND

ii   Now do the same with the following poem, written at about the same time, and compare the mental attitude portrayed with that of the first.

Memorial Tablet
(GREAT WAR)

Squire nagged and bullied till I went to fight.
(Under Lord Derby's Scheme) I died in hell –
(They called it Passchendaele). My wound was slight,
And I was hobbling back; and then a shell
Burst slick upon the duck-boards: so I fell
Into the bottomless mud, and lost the light.

At sermon-time, while Squire is in his pew,
He gives my gilded name a thoughtful stare;
For, though low down upon the list, I'm there;
'*In proud and glorious memory*' . . . that's my due.
Two bleeding years I fought in France, for Squire;
I suffered anguish that he's never guessed.
Once I came home on leave: and then went west . . .
What greater glory could a man desire?

                                                Siegfried Sassoon

iii   Which of the two poems do you feel more in sympathy with?

b   How would you describe the typical qualities of mind of the following?

    i   poets
    ii   gamblers
    iii   puritans
    iv   fanatics
    v   sceptics
    vi   idealists
    vii   mystics

c   To what extent do the following exist mainly in the mind and to what extent do they have an existence outside the human mind?

    i   culture
    ii   paranormal phenomena e.g. ghosts, poltergeists
    iii   religion
    iv   love

3 DREAMS (see Study Notes, page 150)

DREAMS DREAMS

a   Researchers have divided dreams into three main categories: *pleasure-dreams*, which are self-explanatory, *anxiety dreams* which usually involve some unpleasant experience, perhaps repeated or continued over a series of dreams, and leaving the dreamer feeling disorientated and upset; and, lastly, *lucid dreams* which might be either enjoyable or otherwise but which differ from other types of dreams in that the dreamer is always aware that it is only a dream that a separate self is experiencing and from which s/he can easily extricate her/himself.

  i   Can you tell the group about any pleasure dreams you have had?

  ii Do you have anxiety dreams now, or did you have them when you were a child?

  iii There is another category of anxiety dream that might be called the professional anxiety dream – for example actors dream about forgetting their lines and a teacher may dream s/he cannot find the room s/he is supposed to be teaching in until the last five minutes of the lesson. This is repeated for six consecutive lessons. Have you ever had a dream like that?

  iv Some people maintain that analysis of our dreams can tell us a very great deal about our personalities and preoccupations, and others believe that dreams can actually predict the future. For example the great Swiss psychologist C. G. Jung had a series of dreams just before the outbreak of the First World War that seemed to be a portent of what was to come. Have you any experience of or opinions about this?

Some interpretations

Losing teeth: Means you might be going to lose a friend

A nun: A windfall

A pig: Suggests extravagance

Wearing ragged old clothes: Success in business

Falling: Is said to mean a fear of losing control of our lives

Ocean: Someone close to you is being disloyal

Tunnel: Suggests frustration

DISCUSSING DAYDREAMS

B   DAYDREAMS (see Study Notes, page 150)

Books on thinking tend to concentrate on such topics as problem-solving, logical reasoning and decision-making and neglect the much more common activity of daydreaming which, it is reliably estimated, takes up to 40% of some people's lives. It is not, as some people think, a waste of time because it satisfies the need of the human mind to be filled with thought, with the result that children who daydream a lot tend to be happier and even have better concentration than those with less active imaginations.

Here are some actual daydreams:

'Usually "the grass is greener" variety in my case – exotic places, empty beaches . . . anything but work . . . .'

'I sometimes run through conversations with people. It might be a conversation I've already had or one I'm shortly going to have or an entirely imaginary one. If it's the first kind it's often because I realise something went wrong in the conversation and I want to put it right.'

'Sometimes I start thinking I'm in the wrong job, and should be doing something entirely different on the other side of the world!'

    i   What are the common themes of your daydreams and how would you explain them?

    ii   Which situation do you find most conducive to daydreaming? Are you always alone when you daydream? Can you daydream while driving or while listening to somebody talking?

    iii   Some people defend daydreaming as a necessary and even creative activity that exercises and develops the imagination, and others regard it as psychologically dangerous in that it offers a retreat from reality and a substitute for action. What's your opinion? Does Walter Mitty (Text B) take it too far?

4   CONNOTATIONS (see Study Notes, page 150)

A connotation is the suggesting of a meaning by a word apart from the thing it explicitly names or describes (*Webster's New Collegiate Dictionary*). To give an example, a Rolls Royce is a large powerful car made in Derby, England, but its connotations are of extreme luxury, film stars, royalty, elegant living etc.

a   What are the connotations of the following in your opinion?

i	red roses	vi	the colour white
ii	Las Vegas	vii	Paris
iii	shaved heads for men	viii	long hair for men
iv	Oxbridge	ix	snakes
v	lions	x	Hollywood

RELATING DREAMS

b   Can you suggest any more of your own?

c   Which connotations or associations do advertisements for the following typically use to sell the products or services concerned?
   i   perfumes
   ii cars

C LISTENING ACTIVITIES

There are many obstructions to accurate listening and interpretation. To prevent communication breakdowns we must be aware of what we have in our minds and on our minds. In our minds we have preconceived ideas, assumptions and prejudices based on our cultural conditioning. Naturally, we tend to interpret meaning on the grounds of our own experience. Look at these two words:

| Come here |

1   What is their function?
a   To command?
b   To lure?
c   To suggest?
d   To invite?
e   To comfort?

2   What does interpretation depend on?

3   Now listen to five mini-dialogues and answer the questions in numerals.

4   Stress on particular words and intonation are attitude indicators and may give the most accurate impression of what is really in the mind.

a   Listen to these responses (i)–(v), paying particular attention to stress and intonation. Write the stimulus which could have prompted the response.

b   Compare your answers with those of other students and note any differences.

D STRUCTURE AND LANGUAGE USAGE (see Study Notes, page 150)

1   Make new sentences of approximately the same meaning, using the words given after each sentence.

   a   Robert didn't actually know the last word, but he was able to work it out from the rest of the crossword.
      i   deduce   ii   deducible

   b   A link has been discovered between the incidence of some hormonal problems and participation in long-distance races.
      i   correlate   ii   correlation   iii   posit

   c   NASA scientists working on ice-covered lakes in Antarctica have concluded that sufficient heat and gas would have been trapped beneath the surface of Mars to have generated living organisms.
      i   deduce   ii   conclusion   iii   postulate

   d   The tax authorities came to the conclusion that a tax avoidance scheme was being operated when valuable investments were moved abroad.
      i   inference   ii   conclude

   e   A recently published survey of 700 localities in London suggests that material deprivation and ill-health are closely linked.
      i   correlate   ii   causal connection

   f   Reading between the lines of the advertisement, Jane decided they were looking for someone younger.
      i   infer   ii   imply

2   Match one of the phrases to one of the sentences below. Then change the sentence to include that phrase (in another form if necessary) to make a new sentence of approximately the same meaning.
   get the idea; bear in mind; slip one's mind; cross one's mind; give one/some/an approximate/a rough idea; have in mind; have an idea; bring to mind; change one's mind; be uppermost in one's mind; call to mind

   a   Sorry, I completely *forgot* about it.
   b   What exactly *do you want*?
   c   I don't think he *knows anything* about this kind of work.
   d   Her sculptures *remind me* of Giacometti.
   e   *Don't forget* that he's very new to the job.
   f   I'm sorry, it just *didn't occur* to me that you'd want to come.
   g   They've somehow *gained the impression* that you're there to help them.
   h   I *don't want* to buy those books now. Would you mind taking them back?
   i   Financial matters were obviously *their main concern*.

3 WHAT'S ON THEIR MINDS?

a We often prepare the way for invitations, requests etc. by asking a question before making the actual invitation or request, and therefore when native speakers hear the first question they are automatically alerted to the imminence of the invitation. Look at the examples and then discuss different ways of completing the remaining three-part exchanges.

Example: Do you like ice-skating?
Yes, I used to do quite a lot.
Like to come this weekend sometime?

Example: Doing anything on the weekend 15th–17th April, Mark?
Not as far as I know.
Only there's a conference one of us ought to cover.

i How are you off for cash, Peter? (friends at work)
Not too badly.
....

ii Got anything arranged for the weekend? (two female friends)
Nothing very definite – why?
....

iii Will you be needing the car on Saturday night, Dad?
No, ...
....

iv How do you like Hamburg, Robert? (Export Sales Manager to member of his team)
....
....

b Prepare and practise similar three-part exchanges on the following subjects.

i A concert of Vivaldi's music.
ii A meeting with a business client in Jeddah.
iii An informal invitation to dinner at your home.
iv Three hours' extra work after normal working hours to get something finished.

E WRITING ACTIVITIES

1

a Look again at section B1 (page 140). Write a short essay (minimum 200 words) on one of the following in relation to a field of study you are particularly interested in:

  i   The various intellectual fashions that have come and gone in recent years.

  ii The very latest developments and how they are likely to affect the subject in the future.

b Refer back to section B2 (page 141). Write an account of a dream or nightmare you have had.

2 EXTENSION WORK

Often when we write a piece of prose we have an idea at the back of our mind that influences our choice of language. For obvious reasons the writer of the following is treating the room he describes as a kind of container.

'You can hardly get into my son's room, it is full of his possessions *crammed* into every inch of the available space: there are 50% more books *squeezed into* the bookcases than there is really *room for* and every drawer, every cupboard is *full to overflowing* with papers, books and sports equipment, with the result that there isn't *enough room* for essentials such as clothes and shoes which have to be *stored* in various other parts of the house, much to everybody's annoyance.'

However, it may be less obvious that the writer of an obituary can write about a famous man's life in the same way:

'. . . Professor Graham led a marvellously *full* life, *crammed* with hard work, discoveries in several academic fields, and *full to overflowing* with the satisfaction of an unusually happy family life. In fact Jack Graham's life *contained* enough to *fill* three ordinary lives and *had no room* whatsoever for the petty rivalries and jealousies that *occupy* the minds of lesser men . . .'

  a All the following can be written about as containers. Write about six to ten lines describing a particular example of each, using the container vocabulary *italicised* in the passages above.

   i   a lecture   ii a holiday   iii somebody's mind

3 TEXT IMPROVEMENT

Problems often occur when we mix the guiding ideas (the metaphors). For example the following text, written by a student of English, is a mixture of the typical terminology used for describing plant life, seamanship, competition racing and politics, all in one short paragraph, producing an effect of confusion.

'When you are to *produce* a theory you should take care that the *starting-point* is a good one. It must be *well anchored* so that it can *hold* the *superstructure* of logical argumentation without *breaking up*. Even if the *basis* is only slightly *off-balance* it may still result in the *overthrow* of part or all of your theory.'

In fact theories or arguments are often described in terms of the construction of a building. Study the 'construction terms' in the following passage and then improve the above text by replacing the *italicised* words with the 'construction terms'.

When we construct a building we first have to make absolutely sure that the foundations are sufficiently sound and strong to support the main framework of the building without collapsing. The slightest shakiness in the foundations can result in the collapse of part or all of the building.

4   Notice how the following describes a lecturer's seminars in terms of a journey:

'I find his seminars never really get *anywhere*: he *starts off* with great enthusiasm and *covers a lot of ground* in a very short time, but after a while you begin to realise that *he's left most of his* audience *behind* and that he's either *going round in circles* or *gone off at a complete tangent* and *completely lost his way*.'

Describe a film, play or novel in similar terms.

STUDY NOTES

B1   ACADEMIC DISCIPLINES

Useful vocabulary for discussion

a   investigate; discover; gain an understanding of; seek to explain; the way (the human mind) works; motivation; interaction; behaviour; psychiatry; educationalists; criminology; social psychology

   the economy, distribution; goods and services; consumption; money/financial markets; supply and demand; international trade; exchange rates; inflation; Keynesian policies; monetarist policies; balance of payments; interaction between . . .; the Treasury (UK and US); business schools; long-term economic planning origins; development; evolution; genesis; environment; tool-making; development of language; social organisation; religious forms; socialisation; civilisation; primitive societies

   sentence structure; the rules governing the way words are combined; communication; linguistic phenomena; historical linguistics; descriptive linguistics (concentrating on describing a particular language system); contrastive linguistics (focusing on differences between languages; especially as input for language teaching); phonology; syntax development; language learning; bilingualism; speech defects

   motion; interaction; matter; energy; mechanics; relativity; thermodynamics; nuclear physics; astrophysics

b   pure; scientific method; induction; controlled experiments; observation

e   intuition; an analytical mind; a talent for patient observation and experimentation; a capacity for highly abstract thought; a good head for mathematics; mental stamina

B2 ATTITUDES AND QUALITIES OF MIND

Useful vocabulary for discussion

a i romanticism; patriotism; jingoism (extreme patriotism); a romantic view of . . .
ii critical; bitterness; pointless; pointlessness; to be conned into something (colloquial)
b strict; self-denying; single-minded; otherworldly; doubting; indifferent to danger/risk etc.; spiritually enlightened; prophetic; detached

B3 DREAMS

The past continuous tense is very useful for descriptions of this kind.

Useful vocabulary for discussion

a I felt I was floating across . . .; I felt as if I was falling; I was being dragged along corridors towards . . .; I was shouting out for help . . .; I'm in a plane over mountains and . . .; It was as if I . . .

b DAYDREAMS

I imagine I'm lying on a beach . . .; I start/get to (colloquial) thinking about what it would be like if . . .; fantasise; make plans; mull over (colloquial = keep thinking about, especially when trying to make a decision); to go over; keep thinking about

B4 CONNOTATIONS

Useful vocabulary for discussion

suggests; brings to mind; makes one think of; carries the suggestion of . . .

D1 STRUCTURE AND LANGUAGE USAGE

Study the following sentences and use the information they provide to complete D1.

I *inferred* from the company report that all was not well in the Boardroom.

A *correlation* between lung cancer and smoking was established about 25 years ago. (The incidence of lung cancer and smoking were first *correlated* about 25 years ago.)

The Sales Manager *implied* that this would be make-or-break year.

Some scientists have *posited/postulated* a link between leukaemia and the presence of radon in the earth's crust.

What did you *deduce* from her remarks?

I thought she was hinting that we should change our approach.

9
STUDY NOTES

10 NOT QUITE CLEAR

Controversies, ambiguities and wordplay, clarification, jargon, misunderstandings and confusions

A READING TEXTS

1 READING

See Unit 1, Section A (page 5) for instructions. Text B for this unit will be found on page 185.

Text A

COMPUTER SOFTWARE FOR WORKING WITH LANGUAGE by Terry Winograd

In the popular mythology the computer is a mathematics machine: it is designed to do numerical calculations. Yet it is really a language machine: its fundamental power lies in its ability to manipulate linguistic tokens – symbols to which meaning has been assigned. Indeed, 'natural language' (the language people speak and write, as distinguished from the 'artificial' languages in which computer programs are written) is central to computer science. Much of the earliest work in the field was aimed at breaking military codes, and in the 1950s efforts to have computers translate text from one natural language into another led to crucial advances, even though the goal itself was not achieved. Work continues on the still more ambitious project of making natural language a medium in which to communicate with computers.

Science fiction is populated by robots that converse as if they were human, with barely a mechanical tinge to their voice. Real attempts to get computers to converse have run up against great difficulties, and the best of the laboratory prototypes are still a pale reflection of the linguistic competence of the average child.

The prospect that text might be translated by a computer arose well before commercial computers were first manufactured. In 1949, when the few working computers were all in military laboratories, the mathematician Warren Weaver, one of the pioneers of communication theory, pointed out that the techniques developed for code breaking might be applicable to machine translation.

The programs yielded translations so bad that they were incomprehensible. The problem is that natural language does not embody meaning in the same way that a cryptographic code embodies a message. The meaning of a sentence in a natural language is dependent not only on the form of the sentence but also on the context. One can see this most clearly through examples of ambiguity.

In the simplest form of ambiguity, known as lexical ambiguity, a single word has more than one possible meaning. Thus 'Stay away from the bank' might be advice to an investor or to a child too close to a river.

In a structural ambiguity the problem goes beyond a single word. Consider the sentence 'He saw that gasoline can explode'. It has two interpretations based on quite different uses of 'that' and 'can'. Hence the sentence has two possible grammatical structures, and the translator must choose between them . . .

An ambiguity of 'deep structure' is subtler still: two readings of a sentence can have the same apparent grammatical structure but nonetheless differ in meaning. 'The chickens are ready to eat' implies that something is about to eat something, but which are the chickens?

A fourth kind of ambiguity – semantic ambiguity – results when a phrase can play different roles in the overall meaning of a sentence. The sentence 'David wants to marry a Norwegian' is an example. In one meaning of the sentence the phrase 'a Norwegian' is referential. David intends to marry a particular person, and the speaker of the sentence has chosen an attribute of the person – her being from Norway – in order to describe her. In another meaning of the sentence the phrase is attributive. Neither David nor the speaker has a particular person in mind; the sentence simply means that David hopes to marry someone of Norwegian nationality.

A fifth kind of ambiguity might be called pragmatic ambiguity. It arises from the use of pronouns and special nouns such as 'one' and 'another'. Take the sentence 'When a bright moon ends a dark day, a brighter one will follow.' A brighter day or a brighter moon? At times it is possible for translation software to simply translate the ambiguous pronoun or noun, thereby preserving the ambiguity in the translation. In many cases, however, this strategy is not available. In a Spanish translation of 'She dropped the plate on the table and broke it' one must choose either the masculine 'lo' or the feminine 'la' to render 'it'. The choice forces the translator to decide whether the masculine 'plato' (plate) or the feminine 'mesa' (table) was broken.

In many ambiguous sentences the meaning is obvious to a human reader, but only because the reader brings to the task an understanding of context. Thus 'The porridge is ready to eat' is unambiguous because one knows porridge is inanimate. 'There's a man in the room with a green hat on' is unambiguous because one knows rooms do not wear hats. Without such knowledge virtually any sentence is ambiguous.

Adapted from Terry Winograd, *Scientific American*, December 1984

2 QUESTIONS ON THE TEXTS

TEXT A

a   What do you think the following items from the text mean?

  i   'two readings of a sentence'
  ii   'this strategy is not available'
  iii 'a pale reflection of'
  iv   'virtually any'
  v   'translation software'
  vi   'manipulate linguistic tokens' (This looks difficult but is partly explained in the text.)

b   Do you think computer translation is desirable and/or possible?

TEXT B

a   Have you had any similar experience of the phenomenon described in the text? Tell the rest of the group.

b   How do such misunderstandings occur in your experience?

c   Are they an inevitable part of human communication or can something be done to eradicate them?

B   COMMUNICATIVE ACTIVITIES

1   MORE DETAILS (see Study Notes, page 165)

a

Consider the following situations and say what would need further clarification. Then discuss what language would be used to ask for that clarification.

  i   Your company invites you to go on a five-day business trip to Kuwait. Normally the General Manager prefers to go on these trips.
  ii   Your eleven-year-old twins come home from school asking to go on a week's school trip to France at Easter.
  iii At a job interview the conversation has concentrated so far on your qualifications and background and what the company in general expects of its employees.
  iv   A young woman knocks on your door and asks for money for a charity you have never heard of.
  v   You're having difficulty finding a secretary, and a friend says they know just the person for the job.
  vi   There are rumours about a 'structural reorganisation' of your company as a response to falling profits. The General Manager calls a meeting of executives.

b NOT THE WHOLE STORY

In which way do the following avoid telling the whole story? Discuss what they don't tell us.

    i   holiday brochures

    ii   political speeches

    iii   obituaries and epitaphs

    iv   job descriptions

    v   advertisements for real estate

2 WHERE DO WE DRAW THE LINE? (see Study Notes, page 165)

A lot of people are not at all sure what their solution would be for the following contemporary controversies. Read the two sides of each controversy, and then discuss where the line should be drawn, stating any doubts you have about the possibility of deciding.

a   i   A child must have a framework of imposed activity and discipline within which to develop. A child must take second place in adult society, taking the centre stage only when invited to. 'Spare the rod and spoil the child' is as true as ever today.

    ii   Children need freedom to develop! Like flowers, they need air and space to grow, so don't cage them with your little rules or overburden them with your preparations for the adult world. Let them play and dream! Harsh reality will teach its dull lesson soon enough!

b   i   The reason we go to work is to provide financial support for ourselves and our family. It is a means to an end, often extremely enjoyable and occasionally painful. To let it take us over is to endanger everything we hold most dear.

    ii   Our work is an end in itself. Give yourself unstintingly and it will give to you generously in return. Consider the Company as your family that needs your total loyalty and commitment and not just on a nine-to-five basis.

c   i   The purpose of a university is to train young people for responsible positions in industry, commerce, the professions, local and national government etc. Its *raison d'être* is servicing the wider community, not sharpening the perceptions of the scholar–hermit in his ivory tower!

    ii   A university is not the servant of the state but of truth. That truth is just as likely to be discovered in Sanskrit, philosophy or theology as in the so-called useful subjects of physics, mathematics or engineering. Who was it said 'the purpose of education was to create critics of society'?

d i Most of the jobs traditionally done by men can be done equally satisfactorily by women. With the right social attitudes and arrangements – by which I mean such things as crèches, nursery provision, maternity leave, or job sharing – a job can perfectly well be combined with childrearing and normal family life, to everybody's, including the husband's, benefit.

ii A woman's place is in the home. Of course, women can do all these jobs – soldiers if you like, that isn't the point at issue; the point is whether a woman can do that at no cost to her family. The evidence is that when they neglect their duties as wives and mothers chaos and unhappiness are the inevitable consequences.

e i The disadvantaged in society feel they have a right to state financial support sufficient for the maintenance of a reasonable standard of living. State benefits for the unemployed, for example, should be close to the average wage.

ii The politicians of some parties feel that if this is done the unemployed won't bother to find work. It is only by keeping down benefits to an absolute minimum that the recipients will make the effort to do something about their situation.

f i Don't trouble yourself about this vale of tears called *life*. What is it but a rather chaotic rehearsal for something better, a preparation for the real thing, not itself the real thing. So be patient!

   ii You've only got one life, so enjoy it while you can. Treat each day as if it is your last on this earth, squeezing the last drops of life from it. Eat, drink and be merry, for tomorrow you die.

3 What are the controversies that surround the following?

a The peaceful applications of nuclear energy
b euthanasia
c test-tube babies.

4 The following pairs or groups of qualities often merge with each other at a certain point. For example *courage* might become *recklessness* and *foolishness* when the risks are so great that failure is inevitable. At which point do the following merge?

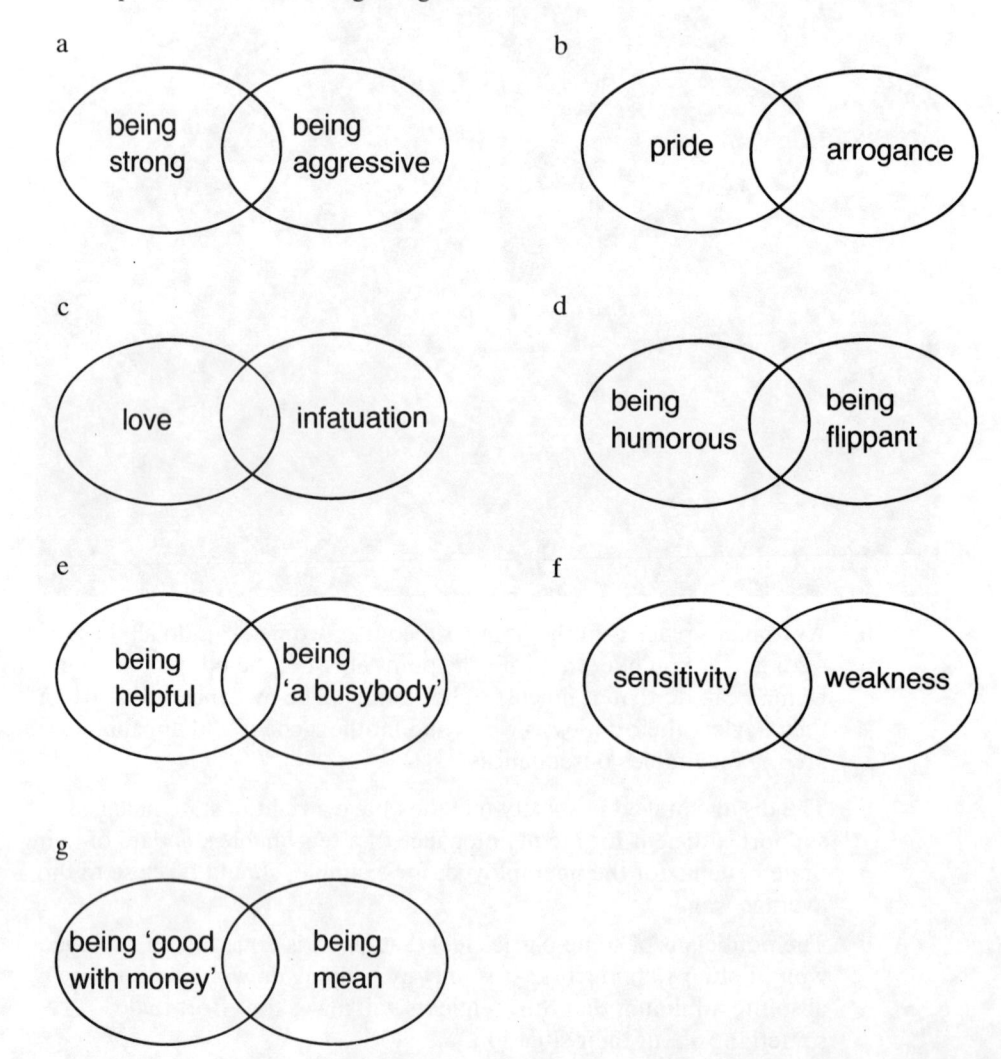

a being strong / being aggressive

b pride / arrogance

c love / infatuation

d being humorous / being flippant

e being helpful / being 'a busybody'

f sensitivity / weakness

g being 'good with money' / being mean

TALKING ABOUT HUMAN QUALITIES

5 'INTER-COMMUNICATING METHODOLOGISTS'
(see Study Notes, page 166)

a   Read the following job advertisement (*Guardian*, early April 1986) and give the meanings of the following terms:

   i   informally structured (line 2)   v   ongoing (9)
   ii   co-ordination and liaison (5)   vi   generate (9)
   iii interaction (6)   vii module (16)
   iv   feedback (8)   viii normative (17)

Advanced Liaison Unit

Inter-communicating Methodologists

West Midlands MCC require experienced persons to act in a general capacity, the work being 1
informally structured and hours adaptable to suit the mutual interests of the person
and the unit.

Initially tenable over a four-year rolling contract period the posts are designed to fill a need in
the administrative services offered by the council in the fields of co-ordination and liaison 5
generally, but with scope for further development as the opportunities for interaction both
within and without departmental boundaries expand to take account of new circumstances
and challenges arising from feedback in the community at large.

Within an essentially experimental framework it is hoped to generate ongoing programmes
with sufficient flexibility to enable both established personnel and new entrants to harmoni- 10
cally interact with a view to analysing work-load definitions as they arise, and in particular to
consolidate what has been achieved in order to balance the need for initiating future projects
with the desirability where possible of expansion "in-house" of proven existing case experience. With their emphasis on complementarity, duties are expected to be integrative, although
individual disciplinary insights will be welcome where they can contribute effectively to a 15
more heterogeneous and cross-sectional evaluation of the work as perceived in the module as
a whole. Normative concepts will thus be largely deemed coterminous with rather than distinct from functional ones with the intention of creating a novel, creative, and explorative
context as the basis for further innovation.

The unit is an Equal Opportunities Employer and encourages applications regardless of age, 20
colour, race, creed, disability, intelligence, gender, marital status or sexual orientation. No
straight Wasps need apply.

---

b   Do you have a clear idea of what the job entails or do some areas of the text require clarification? Which?

6 MORE THAN ONE MEANING

Here are some examples of sentences with more than one meaning. In some of the examples this is intentional (e.g. vii), in some quite accidental (e.g. iii, iv and ix) and in some it depends on pronunciation.

a   Give two possible meanings for each sentence.

b   Give the *reason* for the ambiguity.

c   Where possible, change the sentence to remove the ambiguity.

   i   Wife and mother of a teenage son . . .
   ii   Sixty minute cleaners.
   iii Asked about a report that cracks had appeared in the recently-built extension to the M23, a County Council spokesman said it was completely without foundation. (newspaper item)
   iv   Jane is the woman on the left of Richard.
   v   It's too hot to eat.
   vi   Only gym shoes to be worn.
   vii Have a go at TV. (An invitation by Channel 4 television for viewers to express their opinions on programmes actually on television.)
   viii I had a boyfriend once but someone poached him.
   ix   On the quayside there were soldiers kissing their wives and girlfriends goodbye.
   x   When I got up this morning my bedroom was full of aeroplanes – I had left the landing light on.

AMBIGUITY, WORDPLAY etc

7 INTENTIONAL AMBIGUITY IN ADVERTISEMENTS

Look at the following advertisements and say how they use ambiguity or wordplay.

a

sinclair

Now you can watch a little TV anywhere

b

Money needn't be a wait on your mind.

c

SEE THE ECONOMY BREAKDOWN ON PAGE 5712

d

This is a plug for **KINGS ELECTRICAL** NEW SHOP *Opening Tuesday 12th February. Many opening offers.*

AMBIGUITY IN ADVERTISEMENTS

C LISTENING ACTIVITIES

1. Listen to the following account of a sea expedition. As you listen, mark the statements you feel certain of with a T for true, or an F for false, using a pencil. Don't worry should you not be able to decide on all the statements at first hearing, as you will be given another chance. Remember: if the statement is not completely true, mark it false.

   a The ship was chartered by a biologist.
   b The scientist was born in the North Country.
   c The ship was headed for New Guinea.
   d An albatross was sighted.
   e The scientist asked permission to kill the bird.
   f The crew protested because they were superstitious.
   g The captain gave permission to shoot the bird.
   h Seven mishaps occurred as a result of the killing of the bird.
   i There were three engine failures.
   j The net caught on the bottom of the boat.
   k The captain fell overboard as a result of the storm.
   l Jackie Larson broke his rib.
   m The scientist became seasick again.
   n The ship was forced to land.
   o The cook decided to look for other employment.

2. Discuss with other members of the class:

   a What assumptions were made? Why?
   b How did these assumptions affect your answers?
   c How often do assumptions based on ambiguity and interpretation occur in everyday life? Give examples from your own experience.

D STRUCTURE AND LANGUAGE USAGE (see Study Notes, page 166)

1. Make new sentences from the following, using the items underneath and expressing more or less the same meaning.

   a It's possible that the share boom is bottoming out.
      i may   ii possibility   iii might well
   b Perhaps French involvement in the Middle East has triggered these attacks.
      i might   ii arguably   iii could/possibly
   c There's a possibility that student grants will eventually be replaced by student loans.
      i may   ii possibly   iii conceivable

d   Perhaps she was turned down because of her outspokenness regarding company policy.
    i   could   ii   might   iii   presumably
e   Some university philosophy departments may have to be closed.
    i   chance   ii   on the cards (colloquial)   iii   stage/reach

2   Match the sentences below with one of the items in the box. Then make a new sentence incorporating the new word, keeping more or less the same meaning. Sometimes there is more than one possibility.

confuse/confusion	obscure (verb)	
mix up (verb)/mix-up (noun)	distort/distortion	fudge (verb)

a   The Treasury says the monthly figures are untypical because of the three days of national holiday.
b   Of course it was an interesting talk, but I felt it didn't sufficiently separate description from explanation.
c   The ministers have had serious disagreements, but they will no doubt produce a form of words suggesting peace and harmony at the end.
d   I think what happened was that some of the letters were sent to the wrong addresses.
e   All this empty verbiage prevented people from seeing the real problem.
f   I don't think many people actually knew what the purpose of the meeting was.

3   MISUNDERSTANDINGS (see Study Notes, page 166)

Read the following and then make a sentence about the misunderstanding, using the items below.

a   US President Coolidge invited a group of country friends to the White House. They were not used to such surroundings, and so they self-consciously copied everything the President did. He poured half his coffee into his saucer and so did they, he added cream and sugar and they did the same. Then they were surprised to see the President put his saucer on the floor for his cat.
    i   realise   ii   impression   iii   think

b   A note was thrown from the window of a train as it went through a station: 'Mr Richards of St Albans, Hertfordshire has left the kettle on the cooker. Please inform the police.' The police called and found the kettle on the cooker, but the gas had not been lit.
    i   assume   ii   realise/forget   iii   remember

c   Wine gums have been renamed soft fruit gums for export to Saudi Arabia because the Saudis thought they contained alcohol.
    i   expect   ii   mistaken   iii   misapprehension

IDENTIFYING MISUNDERSTANDINGS   PAST PERFECT

d The Finance Director went to a working breakfast with a foreign client, but the client failed to turn up. In fact he had cancelled. The Finance Director's secretary had left a message to that effect on her boss's answerphone, which he hadn't played back.

   i assume   ii think   iii foresee

e Paul invited Debbie to a party thinking he was dating her, whereas she thought they were going as two singles and that Paul wanted a lift home because the party was some distance away.

   i idea   ii impression   iii take

4 WHAT DO YOU MEAN EXACTLY? (see Study Notes, page 166)

In the following examples the questioner is either asking what a particular term means because s/he doesn't know (e.g. a), or is asking in which sense a common word with several meanings is being used (e.g. b), or asking the speaker to elaborate on what s/he has said (e.g. c).

Look at the examples and suggest contexts for (c), (d), (f), (g) and (i). Then complete the exchanges with an appropriate request for clarification from B.

a A Natural language is central to computer science. (Text A)
    B ....?
    A The language people speak and write, as distinct from artificial computer languages.

b A 'For me the key word is belief.'
    B ....?
    A 'Er . . . in the sense of belief in oneself, self-confidence if you like.'

c A 'I thought it was all a bit over the top.'
    B ....?
    A 'The characters were just grotesque caricatures.'

d A 'He's got to be a self-starter.'
    B ....?
    A 'Someone who won't keep coming back with a lot of silly questions, who'll just get on with it.'

e A It promises much greater cost-effectiveness.
    B ....?
    A Because ultimately it will lead to cheaper raw materials and lower unit costs.

f A 'I'm not sure about the holiday any more.'
    B ....?
    A 'Well, we don't seem to be getting on too well, do we?'

g A 'I must admit he does try to get others going a bit sometimes.'
    B ....?
    A 'For example, he'll whisper remarks to the others or jab them with something.'

ASKING FOR CLARIFICATION

h A 'I'm getting a bit tired of all this nonsense.'
    B ....?
    A 'Well, it's so repetitive, isn't it? Nothing ever changes.'

i A Substantive progress has been made.
    B ....?
    A The two sides are talking the same language, and an agenda for next week's meeting has been agreed.

E WRITING ACTIVITIES

1 DIFFERENT INTERPRETATIONS

Read the following text on the different interpretations of a problem that the various people involved might make and then write similar short texts based on the facts outlined below.

    Suppose that a student reported himself as feeling tired and listless, generally not very well, and that he did not feel he could be bothered to do anything. A students' union officer might conclude that the student's problem was depression, and might probe to find out more about the depression by asking the student how long it had been going on. The doctor at the university medical centre might say that the problem was a cold, that there were a lot of them about and that she had just had one herself. The student's academic tutor might think that the student was not absorbing himself sufficiently in his work, and that a bit more application and hard work would make still more application and hard work easier. The campus radical might think that the problem was classical anomie and alienation, brought on by the death throes of the capitalist system, and the student counsellor might start from the belief that the problem must lie with the student's sex life. Each of these people finds a different problem in the situation, at least in part because they are each inclined to attribute different causes to events.

a   An executive aged 48 at the peak of a highly successful career in top management suddenly turns down an offered promotion and moves with his family to the depths of the country in order to start a small pottery in his back garden and 'live the simple life'.

      Consider interpretations by: the company Chairman/doctor/close friends/wife/children.

b   A 20-year-old wife suffers from persistent depression for over a year after giving birth to her first child.

      Doctor/her mother/her husband/her best friend/her baby.

c   A soldier, married, with four children, applies to be transferred to a non-combatant regiment.

      Wife/commanding officer/best friend/own conscience.

d   Write about something you have done (or are thinking of doing) in your own life that was (or will be) similarly open to several different interpretations.

2 Refer back to section B2 (page 154). Choose one of the controversies and write briefly on it (approximately 150 words) giving both sides of the argument.

3 Look again at Section B3 (page 156). *Either*: Write a similarly vague and indecisive letter of application for the following job. Refer to your particular suitability.

FUND-RAISER
Aid the Ambiguous

This recently founded charity now in its 25th year has half a mind to appoint one or more full-time or part-time Fund-Raiser(s). The Fund-Raiser(s) would work either in the charity's Bridlington headquarters or from another suitable base if one could be found.

The qualities we are almost certainly looking for include, on the one hand, single-minded dedication to the job and, on the other hand, a wide spread of extramural activities. The successful candidate(s) will have definite ideas about how funds should be raised plus a willingness to defer to other points of view.

We are looking for someone under 45 but might prefer candidates over that age.

Salary negotiable in the range £5,000 to £15,000.

Telephone, or perhaps better write.

Or: Write an April Fools' Day joke job advertisement of your own using as many jargon terms from the 'inter-communicating methodologists' advertisement as possible.

STUDY NOTES

B1 MORE DETAILS

Useful language for discussion

a
    i   accommodation; itinerary; brief (noun)
    ii   accompany; supervision; costs
    iii entail (verb); company car; company pension scheme; to report to somebody; promotion prospects
    vi kind of work; kind of charity work
    v   word processor; PA (= Personal Assistant); executive secretary
    vi redundancies; staff cutbacks; closures

B2 WHERE DO WE DRAW THE LINE?

Useful language for discussion

a self-discipline; obedience; 'structured'; respect; character; self-reliant; self-development; imagination; do your own thing; work things out for yourself; cultivate your talents; 'thinking time'

b a 'clockwatcher'; to 'switch off' (= forget everything about your work at the end of the working day); to 'think, eat and sleep work'; to take work home with you (literally); to devote your whole life to your job; a 24-hour job (metaphorically); become a 'company' man; to wind down (= relax) after work; the more you put in the more you get out; you get out what you put in (= if you put more effort into your work you get more job satisfaction out)

c the pursuit of truth; pure knowledge; scholarship as opposed to/in contrast to marketable skills; the cultural heritage; the practical application of knowledge; academic independence; a functional view of education; distinguish between education and training; can fuse/mix up education and professional training; government funding of education; cutbacks; 'a political football' (the subject of political dispute, when it should be beyond politics)

d a change in attitudes; sexist; to combine roles; self-development; choose between motherhood and a career; succeed in a man's world; beat men at their own game; compete on equal terms with men

e on the dole (= receiving unemployment benefit); welfare; social security system; paid for out of taxation; minimum wage; to cushion the effects of unemployment; it's bad enough to be unemployed/made redundant without being totally demoralised as well; a means test; at subsistence level; at poverty level

f the postponement of pleasure; to live in hope; the after life; to live for the future; to savour the moment; to live for the present; to make the most of each day

B3

Useful language for discussion

a nuclear power stations; fossil fuels; pollution; threat to the environment

b to bring a human life to an end; nothing to live for; terminally ill; in pain; when life is not worth living; an act of charity/mercy

c give hope to childless couples; to take the mystique out of childbirth; to obviate the need for surrogate mothers; 'clinical'; 'cold'; ethical argument; medical ethics

B5 'INTER-COMMUNICATING METHODOLOGISTS'

Check that you know the following key vocabulary before reading the text:
adaptable, coordination, liaison, scope, interaction, feedback, generate, ongoing, workload, consolidate, complementary, to integrate, insight, heterogeneous, cross-section, innovation

D1 STRUCTURE AND LANGUAGE USAGE

Study and check the meanings of the following examples and then apply the information they provide when you come to do exercises (D1), (D2) and (D3).

> It's quite *conceivable* that the Right will win the next elections.
> *Presumably* it happened as the result of economic pressures.
> *It's on the cards* that one of their assembly plants will have to be closed down.
> The *stage* might be *reached* where he will feel he will have to resign.
> *Arguably* there were things we could have arranged a lot better.

D2 STRUCTURE AND LANGUAGE USAGE

The fluctuations in the exchange rate have had the effect of *distorting* the balance-of-trade figures.

> There was quite a lot of *confusion* as to which points were on the agenda.
> I was totally *confused* as to what I had to do.
> The real issues have all been *obscured* by the intense publicity.
> No doubt the final agreement will be a *fudge* as usual!
> Aren't you *mixing up* causes and reasons?

D3 MISUNDERSTANDINGS

We were all *mistaken* in thinking she was reliable and efficient.

> The Customs were under the *misapprehension* that it didn't need clearance from them.
> We *assumed* he would let us know when we could collect it, but he didn't.
> Nobody could have *foreseen* that circumstances would change quite so quickly.
> I had the *idea* you were coming tomorrow.
> I think we *took* it that you were coming tomorrow.
> I think we *took* it that you weren't in the mood and that was why you didn't turn up.
> I was under the *impression* that this was how she and her family normally spent their Sundays.

D4 WHAT DO YOU MEAN EXACTLY?

Useful language for discussion

define; give a definition of; stand for; elaborate (on) (verb)

Ways of asking for clarification

In what sense?; In which sense exactly?; Meaning?; How does it do that?; In which way/sense are you using the word?; What do you mean by 'impossible'?; What does that mean?; In what way?; Could you elaborate (on that)?; Why's that, then? (colloquial)

TEXTS B

TEXTS B

1 JOINING

Text B

FRIENDSHIP AT DIFFERENT AGES

We have more friends at some times in our lives than others. Taken over a lifetime, the average for each person is 5.6 friends.

Age 3 to 4 Friendship is mostly about playing and is often based on the proximity of the children's homes.

5 to 6 Children say they are friends with somebody because 'they help me', 'they do things for me' or 'they give me presents'; that is, friendship is based on egocentrism.

8 to 10 Loyalty begins to be an important factor. Friends at this age help each other to develop; the basis is sharing, cooperating and doing things for each other.

Early adolescence Friendship is based on personality development, and many friendships are shortlived because changing personalities no longer support each other.

Late adolescence A friend enables one to develop, to be the kind of person one wants to be. There is a strong need for confidants; at about age 17 the average number of friends is also 17 – the highest ever. Friendship at this age involves trust, admiration, intimacy, loyalty and genuineness, but boys' friendships tend to be less intense than girls'. Having few friends is already associated with psychiatric disorders.

Early 20s This is the peak period for making life-long friendships, and it is also the most 'age exclusive' period of our lives (that is, most time is spent with people of the same age).

Late 20s, early 30s The number of friends drops and the family takes over as the main source of social stimulation. The need for confidants weakens.

40s The number of friends rises again because we are now less worried about what other people think of us. Friendship is based on servicing and helping with the tasks of life. However, many men of this age say they have no close friends.

Post-retirement Close friendships are very important: old people who have confidants are considerably less likely to become mentally disturbed than those who do not.

from *All in the Mind*, John Nicholson & Martin Lucas (eds), Multimedia Publications (UK) Ltd, 1984

2 CONTRASTS

Text B

INTELLIGENCE by John Holt

When we talk about intelligence, we do not mean the ability to get a good score on a certain kind of test, or even the ability to do well in school; these are at best only indicators of something larger, deeper, and far more important. By intelligence we mean a style of life, a way of behaving in various situations, and particularly in new, strange, and perplexing situations. The true test of intelligence is not how much we know how to do, but how we behave when we don't know what to do.

The intelligent person, young or old, meeting a new situation or problem, opens himself up to it; he tries to take in with mind and senses everything he can about it; he thinks about it, instead of about himself or what it might cause to happen to him; he grapples with it boldly, imaginatively, resourcefully, and if not confidently at least hopefully; if he fails to master it, he looks without shame or fear at his mistakes and learns what he can from them. This is intelligence. Clearly its roots lie in a certain feeling about life, and one's self with respect to life. Just as clearly, unintelligence is not what most psychologists seem to suppose, the same thing as intelligence only less of it. It is an entirely different style of behaviour, arising out of an entirely different set of attitudes.

Years of watching and comparing bright children and the not-bright, or less-bright, have shown that they are very different kinds of people. The bright child is curious about life and reality, eager to get in touch with it, embrace it, unite himself with it. There is no wall, no barrier between him and life. The dull child is far less curious, far less interested in what goes on and what is real, more inclined to live in worlds of fantasy. The bright child likes to experiment, to try things out. He lives by the maxim that there is more than one way to skin a cat. If he can't do something one way, he'll try another. The dull child is usually afraid to try at all. It takes a good deal of urging to get him to try even once; if that try fails, he is through.

The bright child is patient. He can tolerate uncertainty and failure, and will keep trying until he gets an answer. When all his experiments fail, he can even admit to himself and others that for the time being he is not going to get an answer. This may annoy him, but he can wait. Very often, he does not want to be told how to do the problem or solve the puzzle he has struggled with, because he does not want to be cheated out of the chance to figure it out for himself in the future. Not so the dull child. He cannot stand uncertainty or failure. To him an unanswered question is not a challenge or an opportunity, but a threat. If he can't find the answer quickly, it must be given to him, and quickly; and he must have answers for everything. Such are the children of whom a second-grade teacher once said, 'But my children like to have questions for which there is only one answer.' They did; and by a mysterious coincidence, so did she.

The bright child is willing to go ahead on the basis of incomplete understanding and information. He will take risks, sail uncharted seas, explore when the landscape is dim, the landmarks few, the light poor. To give only one example, he will often read books he does not understand in the hope that after a while enough understanding will emerge to make it worth while to go on. In this spirit some of my fifth-graders tried to read *Moby Dick*. But the dull child will go ahead only when he thinks he knows exactly where he stands and exactly what an experience will be like, and if it will not be exactly like other experiences he already knows, he wants no part of it. For a while the bright child feels that the universe is, on the whole, a sensible, reasonable, and trustworthy place, the dull child feels that it is senseless, unpredictable, and treacherous. He feels that he can never tell what may happen, particularly in a new situation, except that it will probably be bad.

from *How Children Fail*, John Holt, Delacorte Press, 1982

3 LOGICAL RELATIONS

Text B

THE ORIGIN OF THE SOLAR SYSTEM by E. J. Ewington and D. F. Moore

As Earth is one of the nine planets of the solar system, its origin must be linked with the origin of the solar system. There are, however, several current theories attempting to explain this origin.

a Jeans and Jeffreys suggested the Tidal Hypothesis that the planets and their satellites were originally all part of the sun around which they now revolve. They suggest that a star passed so close to the sun that its attraction caused a bulge of gas on its surface, which was dragged into a tidal wave of gas that became detached from the sun. The theory suggests that these detached masses of gas went into orbit around the sun, before slowly cooling to form the planets.

b The English astronomer, R. A. Lyttleton, proposed the Double Star Hypothesis, which suggests that the sun had a companion, a larger star which underwent a violent explosion to form a brilliant star called a supernova. This larger body was propelled into space by the force of the explosion, but some of the fragments of the explosion were captured by the sun's gravitational field and remained behind to form the planets.

c In recent years, the Condensation Hypothesis has been proposed by Harold Urey. This hypothesis suggests that an explosion of a star resulted in a cloud of dust and gases, such as hydrogen and helium. The particles of dust were drawn together by gravitational attraction to form a thin plate-like disc with a solar mass at the centre which revolved on its axis. Eventually the disc separated to form the planets, leaving the solar mass as the sun at the centre. The disc became segmented and dust comprising each segment compacted to produce a planet, such as Earth.

from *Human Biology and Hygiene*, E. J. Ewington and D. F. Moore, Routledge & Kegan Paul, 1971

4 OMISSION

Text B

THE PEDESTRIAN by Ray Bradbury

To enter out into that silence that was the city at eight o'clock of a misty evening in November, to put your feet upon that buckling concrete walk, to step over grassy seams and make your way, hands in pockets, through the silences, that was what Mr Leonard Mead most dearly loved to do. He would stand upon the corner of an intersection and peer down long moonlit avenues of sidewalk in four directions, deciding what way to go, but it really made no difference; he was alone in this world of AD 2053, or as good as alone, and with a final decision made, a path selected, he would stride off, sending patterns of frosty air before him like the smoke of a cigar.

Sometimes he would walk for hours and miles and return only at midnight to his house. And on his way he would see the cottages and homes with their dark windows, and it was not unlike walking through a graveyard where only the faintest glimmers of firefly light appeared in flickers behind the windows. Sudden grey phantoms seemed to manifest upon inner room walls where a curtain was still undrawn against the night, or there were whisperings and murmurs where a window in a tomblike building was still open.

Mr Leonard Mead would pause, cock his head, listen, look, and march on, his feet making no noise on the lumpy walk. For long ago he had wisely changed to sneakers when strolling at night, because the dogs in intermittent squads would parallel his journey with barkings if he wore hard heels, and lights click on and faces appear and an entire street be startled by the passing of a lone figure, himself, in the early November evening.

On this particular evening he began his journey in a westerly direction, towards the hidden sea. There was a good crystal frost in the air; it cut the nose and made the lungs blaze like a Christmas tree inside; you could feel the cold light going on and off, all the branches filled with invisible snow. He listened to the faint push of his soft shoes through autumn leaves with satisfaction, and whistled a cold quiet whistle between his teeth, occasionally picking up a leaf as he passed, examining its skeletal pattern in the infrequent lamplights as he went on, smelling its rusty smell.

'Hello, in there,' he whispered to every house on every side as he moved. 'What's up tonight on Channel 4, Channel 7, Channel 9? Where are the cowboys rushing, and do I see the United States Cavalry over the next hill to the rescue?'

The street was silent and long and empty, with only his shadow moving like the shadow of a hawk in mid-country. If he closed his eyes and stood very still, frozen, he could imagine himself upon the centre of a plain, a wintry, windless Arizona desert with no house in a thousand miles, and only dry river beds, the streets, for company.

'What is it now?' he asked the houses, noticing his wrist-watch. 'Eight-thirty p.m.? Time for a dozen assorted murders? A quiz? A revue? A comedian falling off the stage?'

Was that a murmur of laughter from within a moon-white house? He hesitated, but went on when nothing more happened. He stumbled over a particularly uneven section of sidewalk. The cement was vanishing under flowers and grass. In ten years of walking by night or day, for thousands of miles, he had never met another person walking, not one in all that time.

He came to a cloverleaf intersection which stood silent where two main highways crossed the town. During the day it was a thunderous surge of cars, and gas stations open, a great insect rustling and a ceaseless jockeying for position as the scarab-beetles, a faint incense puttering from their exhausts, skimmed homeward to the far directions. But now these highways, too, were like streams in a dry season, all stone and bed and moon radiance.

He turned back on a side street, circling around towards his home. He was within a block of his destination when the lone car turned a corner quite suddenly and flashed a fierce white cone of light upon him. He stood entranced, not unlike a night moth, stunned by the illumination, and then drawn towards it.

A metallic voice called to him:

'Stand still. Stay where you are! Don't move.'

He halted.

'Put up your hands!'

'But----' he said.

'Your hands up! Or we'll shoot!'

The police, of course, but what a rare, incredible thing; in a city of three million, there was only one police car left, wasn't that correct? Ever since a year ago, 2052, the election year, the force had been cut down from three cars to one. Crime was ebbing; there was no need now for the police, save for this one lone car wandering and wandering the empty streets.

'Your name?' said the police car in a metallic whisper. He couldn't see the men in it for the bright light in his eyes.

'Leonard Mead,' he said.

'Speak up!'

'Leonard Mead!'

'Business or profession?'

'I guess you'd call me a writer.'

'No profession,' said the police car, as if talking to itself. The light held him fixed, like a museum specimen, needle thrust through chest.

'You might say that,' said Mr Mead. He hadn't written in years. Magazines and books didn't sell any more. Everything went on in the tomblike houses at night now, he thought, continuing his fancy. The tombs, ill-lit by television light, where the people sat like the dead, the grey or multicoloured lights touching their faces, but never really touching them.

'No profession,' said the phonograph voice, hissing. 'What are you doing out?'

'Walking,' said Leonard Mead.

'Walking!'

'Just walking,' he said simply, but his face felt cold.

'Walking, just walking, walking?'

'Yes, sir.'

'Walking where? For what?'

'Walking for air. Walking to see.'

TEXT B

4

TEXT B

'Your address!'
'Eleven South Saint James Street.'
'And there is air in your house, you have an air conditioner, Mr Mead?'
'Yes.'
'And you have a viewing screen in your house to see with?'
'No.'
'No?' There was a crackling quiet that in itself was an accusation.
'Are you married, Mr Mead?'
'No.'
'Not married,' said the police voice behind the fiery beam. The moon was high and clear among the stars and the houses were grey and silent.
'Nobody wanted me,' said Leonard Mead with a smile.
'Don't speak unless you're spoken to!'
Leonard Mead waited in the cold night.
'Just walking, Mr Mead?'
'Yes.'
'But you haven't explained for what purpose.'
'I explained; for air, and to see, and just to walk.'
'Have you done this often?'
'Every night for years.'
The police car sat in the centre of the street with its radio throat faintly humming.
'Well, Mr Mead,' it said.
'Is that all?' he asked politely.
'Yes,' said the voice. 'Here.' There was a sigh, a pop. The back door of the police car sprang wide. 'Get in.'
'Wait a minute, I haven't done anything!'
'Get in.'
'I protest!'
'Mr Mead.'
He walked like a man suddenly drunk. As he passed the front window of the car he looked in. As he had expected, there was no one in the front seat, no one in the car at all.
'Get in.'
He put his hand to the door and peered into the back seat, which was a little cell, a little black jail with bars. It smelled of riveted steel. It smelled of harsh antiseptic; it smelled too clean and hard and metallic. There was nothing soft there.
'Now if you had a wife to give you an alibi,' said the iron voice. 'But---'
'Where are you taking me?'
The car hesitated, or rather gave a faint whirring click, as if information, somewhere, was dripping card by punch-slotted card under electric eyes. 'To the Psychiatric Centre for Research on Regressive Tendencies.'
He got in. The door shut with a soft thud. The police car rolled through the night avenues, flashing its dim lights ahead.

They passed one house on one street a moment later, one house in an entire city of houses that were dark, but this one particular house had all of its electric lights brightly lit, every window a loud yellow illumination, square and warm in the cool darkness.

'That's my house,' said Leonard Mead.

No one answered him.

The car moved down the empty river-bed streets and off away, leaving the empty streets with the empty sidewalks, and no sound and no motion all the rest of the chill November night.

from *The Golden Apples of the Sun*, Ray Bradbury, Doubleday Inc., 1953

5 THE GENERAL AND THE PARTICULAR

Text B1

THE REALITY OF TEACHING IN A COMPREHENSIVE SCHOOL IN 1986

I remember distinctly several years back saying to my old German teacher that I was going to teacher training college. He asked me why, and when I said that hopefully they would teach me to teach, he merely laughed. Now, after four years of training and five of teaching, I can begin to see why he found my naivety so amusing.

At training college you are told always to be exceptionally patient and understanding, particularly with less able pupils, but what they don't tell you is that when you give them this special attention and understanding they exhaust and demoralise you by giving you very little in return – no feedback, none of *their* attention and patience. As a result, after a frustrating day teaching largely unreceptive groups, the last thing you feel like doing is preparing the kind of well thought-out and structured lesson that they in particular need.

When I started teaching, I did so with great hopes of helping students make some genuine progress. The reality is that some pupils enter the school at 11 able to read and do elementary arithmetic and leave five years later able to do little more. How would 'tuning into their mind' help? They are only too well aware of their shortcomings, and their sense of failure, their pessimism, inevitably communicates to us, their teachers.

We are told never to stoop to sarcasm; 'the lowest form of wit' we were warned: yet how can you control 28 fifteen-year-olds without metaphorically slapping them back into place in front of their peers? All the other sanctions have been largely taken away from teachers, so how can you justify taking away our last weapon in this unequal struggle – our tongue?

Our lecturers at college emphasised the importance of being adaptable in one's lessons, of improvising, but very often lessons fail not because the teacher has been insufficiently inventive but because the class, with its own deeply ingrained habits of mind, has been incapable of adjusting to the less structured environment of an improvised lesson.

One of the biggest problems of the present time is motivation. However unsatisfactory, the old-fashioned method of telling children that exam success and 'good behaviour' would secure them a worthwhile job, was at least partly successful. That no longer convinces anybody, and yet, desperate to give any encouragement, I have found myself repeating the tired old argument to pupils and trying to believe it myself, only to be reminded by them cynically that nowadays it's not what you know but who you know that will secure them a job. And the teachers I work with? If I think back to the teachers who influenced and motivated me at my own school, the best were often individualistic or even eccentric characters who in the present school system would be passed over for promotion and perhaps even pressured into early retirement both by 'difficult classes' and the general movement toward a grey bureaucratic conformity.

English Teacher in an East Anglian Comprehensive, 1986

Text B2

THE REALITY OF TEACHING IN A COMPREHENSIVE SCHOOL IN 1986

After four years of teaching English, two problems still perplex me: Firstly, where did the educational theorists who wrote all those fine books I read at training-college actually find the children who validated their theories? Certainly none of the children I have taught would have given any support to their ideas, which make the mistake of pre-supposing that children want to learn and that they see a value in learning. The truth is that most teenagers today have a totally utilitarian view of education, so that whereas poetry is seen as an utter waste of time, a functional form-filling exercise is greeted with enthusiasm and tackled with great care.

Secondly, the teaching strategies I studied at college not only pre-supposed a degree of motivation on the part of the pupil that does not in fact exist but also made unrealistic demands on the teacher. In fact to make these teaching methods work would require that the teacher had endless reserves of patience, superhuman energy and no social life whatsoever outside the school. I would have preferred to have been instructed at a more realistic level, particularly in how to set targets which both educate the pupils in a way and about topics that they are predisposed to accept and allow the teacher to maintain his or her sanity.

English teacher in an East Anglian Comprehensive, 1986

6 STANDPOINT

Text B

WHAT I BELIEVE by Bertrand Russell

At the present time the fiercest and most dangerous animal with which human beings have to contend is man, and the dangers arising from purely physical causes have been very rapidly reduced. In the present day, therefore, fear finds little scope except in relation to other human beings, and fear itself is one of the main reasons why human beings are formidable to each other. It is a recognised maxim that the best defence is attack; consequently people are continually attacking each other because they expect to be attacked. Our instinctive emotions are those that we have inherited from a much more dangerous world, and contain, therefore, a larger proportion of fear than they should; this fear, since it finds little outlet elsewhere, directs itself against the social environment, producing distrust and hate, envy, malice, and all uncharitableness. If we are to profit fully by our new-won mastery over nature, we must acquire a more lordly psychology: instead of the cringing and resentful terror of the slave, we must learn to feel the calm dignity of the master. Reverting to the impulses of approach and withdrawal, this means that impulses of approach need to be encouraged, and those of withdrawal need to be discouraged. Like everything else, this is a matter of degree. I am not suggesting that people should approach tigers and pythons with friendly feelings; I am only saying that since tradition grew up in a more dangerous world, the present-day occasions for fear and withdrawal are less numerous than tradition would lead us to suppose.

It is the conquest of nature which has made possible a more friendly and co-operative attitude between human beings, and if rational men co-operated and used their scientific knowledge to the full, they could now secure the economic welfare of all – which was not possible in any earlier period. Life-and-death competition for the possession of fertile lands was reasonable enough in the past, but it has now become a folly. International government, business organisation, and birth control should make the world comfortable for everybody. I do not say that everybody could be as rich as Croesus, but everybody could have as much of this world's goods as is necessary for the happiness of sensible people. With the problem of poverty and destitution eliminated, men could devote themselves to the constructive arts of civilisation – to the progress of science, the diminution of disease, the postponement of death, and the liberation of the impulses that make for joy.

Why do such ideas appear Utopian? The reasons lie solely in human psychology – not in the unalterable parts of human nature, but in those which we acquire from tradition, education, and the example of our environment. Take, first, international government. The necessity for this is patent to every person capable of political thought, but nationalistic passions stand in the way. Each nation is proud of its independence; each nation is willing to fight till the last gasp to preserve its freedom. This, of course, is mere anarchy, and it leads to conditions exactly analogous to those in the feudal ages before the bold, bad barons were forced in the end to submit to the authority of the king. The attitude we have toward foreign nations is one of withdrawal: the foreigner may be all

TEXT B

right in his place, but we become filled with alarm at the thought that he may have any say in our affairs. Each state, therefore, insists upon the right of private war. Treaties, arbitration, Kellogg Peace Pacts, and the rest are all very well as gestures, but everybody knows that they will not stand any severe strain. So long as each nation has its own army and navy and air force it will use them when it gets excited, whatever treaties its government may have signed.

There will be no safety in the world until men have applied to the rules between different states the great principle which has produced internal security – namely, that in any dispute, force must not be employed by either interested party but only by a neutral authority after due investigation according to recognised principles of law. When all the armed forces of the world are controlled by one world-wide authority, we shall have reached the stage in the relations of states which was reached centuries ago in the relations of individuals. Nothing less than this will suffice.

The basis of international anarchy is men's proneness to fear and hatred. This is also the basis of economic disputes; for the love of power, which is at their root, is generally an embodiment of fear. Men desire to be in control because they are afraid that the control of others will be used unjustly to their detriment. The same thing applies in the sphere of sexual morals; the power of husbands over wives and of wives over husbands, which is conferred by the law, is derived from fear of the loss of possession. This motive is the negative emotion of jealousy, not the positive emotion of love. In education the same kind of thing occurs. The positive emotion which should supply the motive in education is curiosity, but the curiosity of the young is severely repressed in many directions – sexual, theological, and political. Instead of being encouraged in the practice of free inquiry, children are instructed in some brand of orthodoxy, with the result that unfamiliar ideas inspire them with terror rather than with interest. All these bad results spring from a pursuit of security – a pursuit inspired by irrational fears; the fears have become irrational, since in the modern world fearlessness and intelligence, if embodied in social organisation, would in themselves suffice to produce security.

The road to Utopia is clear; it lies partly through politics and partly through changes in the individual. As for politics, far the most important thing is the establishment of an international government – a measure which I expect to be brought about through the world government of the United States. As for the individual, the problem is to make him less prone to hatred and fear, and this is a matter partly physiological and partly psychological. Much of the hatred in the world springs from bad digestion and inadequate functioning of the glands, which is a result of oppression and thwarting in youth. In a world where the health of the young is adequately cared for and their vital impulses are given the utmost scope compatible with their own health and that of their companions, men and women will grow up more courageous and less malevolent than they are at present.

Given such human beings and an international government, the world might become stable and yet civilised, whereas, with our present psychology and political organisation, every increase in scientific knowledge brings the destruction of civilisation nearer.

Bertrand Russell, in *What I Believe*, Sidgwick & Jackson, 1985

7 IN THE NEGATIVE

Text B

THE BREADWINNER by Leslie Halward

The parents of a boy of fourteen were waiting for him to come home with his first week's wages.

The mother had laid the table and was cutting some slices of bread and butter for tea. She was a little woman with a pinched face and a spare body, dressed in a blue blouse and skirt, the front of the skirt covered with a starched white apron. She looked tired and frequently sighed heavily.

The father, sprawling inelegantly in an old armchair by the fireside, legs outstretched, was little too. He had watery blue eyes and a heavy brown moustache, which he sucked occasionally.

These people were plainly poor, for the room, though clean, was meanly furnished, and the thick pieces of bread and butter were the only food on the table.

As she prepared the meal, the woman from time to time looked contemptuously at her husband. He ignored her, raising his eyebrows, humming, or tapping his teeth now and then with his finger-nails, making a pretence of being profoundly bored.

'You'll keep your hands off the money,' said the woman, obviously repeating something that she had already said several times before. 'I know what'll happen to it if you get hold of it. He'll give it to me. It'll pay the rent and buy us a bit of food, and not go into the till at the nearest public-house.'

'You shut your mouth,' said the man, quietly.

'I'll not shut my mouth!' cried the woman, in a quick burst of anger. 'Why should I shut my mouth? You've been boss here for long enough. I put up with it when you were bringing money into the house, but I'll not put up with it now. You're nobody here. Understand? Nobody. I'm boss and he'll hand the money to me!'

'We'll see about that,' said the man, leisurely poking the fire.

Nothing more was said for about five minutes.

Then the boy came in. He did not look older than ten or eleven years. He looked absurd in long trousers. The whites of his eyes against his black face gave him a startled expression.

The father got to his feet.

'Where's the money?' he demanded.

The boy looked from one to the other. He was afraid of his father. He licked his pale lips.

'Come on now,' said the man. 'Where's the money?'

'Don't give it to him,' said the woman. 'Don't give it to him, Billy. Give it to me.'

The father advanced on the boy, his teeth showing in a snarl under his big moustache.

'Where's that money?' he almost whispered.

TEXT B

The boy looked him straight in the eyes.

'I lost it,' he said.

'You – what?' cried his father

'I lost it,' the boy repeated.

The man began to shout and wave his hands about.

'Lost it! Lost it! What are you talking about? How could you lose it?'

'It was in a packet,' said the boy, 'a little envelope. I lost it.'

'Where did you lose it?'

'I don't know. I must have dropped it in the street.'

'Did you go back and look for it?'

The boy nodded. 'I couldn't find it,' he said.

The man made a noise in his throat, half grunt, half moan – the sort of noise that an animal would make.

'So you lost it, did you?' he said. He stepped back a couple of paces and took off his belt – a wide, thick belt with a heavy brass buckle. 'Come here,' he said.

The boy, biting his lower lip so as to keep back the tears, advanced, and the man raised his arm. The woman, motionless until that moment, leapt forward and seized it. Her husband finding strength in his blind rage, pushed her aside easily. He brought the belt down on the boy's back. He beat him unmercifully about the body and legs. The boy sank to the floor, but did not cry out.

When the man had spent himself, he put on the belt and pulled the boy to his feet.

'Now you'll get off to bed,' he said.

'The lad wants some food,' said the woman.

'He'll go to bed. Go and wash yourself.'

Without a word the boy went into the scullery and washed his hands and face. When he had done this he went straight upstairs.

The man sat down at the table, ate some bread and butter and drank two cups of tea. The woman ate nothing. She sat opposite him, never taking her eyes from his face, looking with hatred at him. Just as before, he took no notice of her, ignored her, behaved as if she were not there at all.

When he had finished the meal he went out.

Immediately he had shut the door the woman jumped to her feet and ran upstairs to the boy's room.

He was sobbing bitterly, his face buried in the pillow. She sat on the edge of the bed and put her arms about him, pressed him close to her breast, ran her fingers through his disordered hair, whispered endearments, consoling him. He let her do this, finding comfort in her caresses, relief in his own tears.

After a while his weeping ceased. He raised his head and smiled at her, his wet eyes bright. Then he put his hand under the pillow and withdrew a small dirty envelope.

'Here's the money,' he whispered.

She took the envelope and opened it and pulled out a long strip of paper with some figures on it – a ten shilling note and a sixpence.

from 'The Breadwinner', *Forty Short Short Stories* by Leslie Halward, Edward Arnold, 1965

Note: 'a ten shilling note' and a 'sixpence'; these were dropped when Britain adopted decimal currency. They were equivalent to 50p and 2½p.

8 EMPHASIS

Text B

LIFE AND CAREERS ON THE FOOTBALL TERRACES by Peter Marsh

The football terraces provide an alternative career structure – an orderly framework for making progress in the society of the terrace. Unlike careers in the outside world there's no financial reward to be gained. The payoff is in social terms. But the benefits are still tangible and real. To young working class kids for whom school, work or the dole queue offer little in the way of potential for personal achievement, the availability of an alternative world in which to become somebody is attractive. And so, boys of 9, 10, or 11 are drawn to the terraces by the prospect of immediate membership of a society which offers excitement, danger and a tribal sense of belonging. These are the 'novices' or 'little kids' at the start of their apprenticeship.

To older fans, 'novices' are a bit of an embarrassment because they don't really know what they are doing. Their knowledge of the codes of conduct is limited and superficial. But acquisition of appropriate knowledge and skill is made easier by the fact that there is a distinct model to which they are aspiring. The 'model' is the 'hooligan' or, being less emotive, the 'rowdy'. 'Rowdies' are the energetic lads on the terraces. They are the ones who sing and chant the loudest, wear the most extreme forms of 'gear' and run around a lot. They are also the people magistrates describe as 'animals', 'morons' and 'thugs'.

'Rowdies' form the core membership of the terrace culture. Their average age is 15 or 16 and although there are no initiation rites or entry ceremonies – in fact any supporter can join in a superficial sense – the 'men' are separated from the 'boys' in situations which demand specific action. Only by matching up to the standards expected, and by demonstrating commitment to the commonly held values and ideals, can the 'rowdy' hope to be recognised by his peers.

One very favourable role within the rowdy group is that of the fan who aspires to being an 'aggro leader' or, more colloquially, a 'hard-case'. They are the ones who will lead running charges at the opposition fans, both inside and outside the ground, and they will figure prominently in the scuffles which break out. Being a 'hard-case' gets you the best seat on coaches to away matches; 'novices' buy you beers, and other fans show a satisfying deference. Such a position can be held, informally, without bullying or coercion. It does, however, require a certain degree of fearlessness.

The 'hard-case' builds his reputation not by causing serious injury to other people, but by consistently demonstrating a determination to stand up for himself and his group. But his fearlessness is limited. For the total absence of fear is an aspect of character more typical of the 'nutter' than the 'hard-case'. 'Nutters' 'go crazy' or 'go mad' – they go beyond the fans' limits of acceptable and sane behaviour. In doing so, however, everybody else on the terraces comes to

TEXT B

understand more clearly where those limits lie. In fact, the existence of 'nutters' is proof of the existence of order in the first place. If random action was the norm, 'nutters' would be indistinguisable from anybody else. But the fact that they are viewed, from the inside, as deviant, provides us with a very useful way of assessing the nature and extent of the informal terrace rules. We can look at what shouldn't be done, which is always an easier task than teasing out what should.

Peter Marsh, *Football Hooliganism: The Wider Context*, Inter-Action Trust, 1978

9 IN THE MIND

Text B

THE SECRET LIFE OF WALTER MITTY by James Thurber

'We're going through!' The Commander's voice was like thin ice breaking. He wore his full-dress uniform, with the heavily braided white cap pulled down rakishly over one cold gray eye. 'We can't make it, sir. It's spoiling for a hurricane, if you ask me.' 'I'm not asking you, Lieutenant Berg,' said the Commander. 'Throw on the power lights! Rev her up to 8,500! We're going through!' The pounding of the cylinders increased: ta-pocketa-pocketa-pocketa-pocketa-pocketa. The Commander stared at the ice forming on the pilot window. He walked over and twisted a row of complicated dials. 'Switch on No. 8 auxiliary!' he shouted. 'Switch on No. 8 auxiliary!' repeated Lieutenant Berg. 'Full strength in No. 3 turret!' shouted the Commander. 'Full strength in No. 3 turret!' The crew, bending to their various tasks in the huge, hurtling eight-engined Navy hydroplane, looked at each other and grinned. 'The Old Man'll get us through,' they said to one another. 'The Old Man ain't afraid of Hell!' . . .

'Not so fast! You're driving too fast!' said Mrs Mitty. 'What are you driving so fast for?'

'Hmm?' said Walter Mitty. He looked at his wife, in the seat beside him, with shocked astonishment. She seemed grossly unfamiliar, like a strange woman who had yelled at him in a crowd. 'You were up to fifty-five,' she said. 'You know I don't like to go more than forty. You were up to fifty-five.' Walter Mitty drove on toward Waterbury in silence, the roaring of the SN202 through the worst storm in twenty years of Navy flying fading in the remote, intimate airways of his mind. 'You're tensed up again,' said Mrs Mitty. 'It's one of your days. I wish you'd let Dr Renshaw look you over.'

Walter Mitty stopped the car in front of the building where his wife went to have her hair done. 'Remember to get those overshoes while I'm having my hair done,' she said. 'I don't need overshoes,' said Mitty. She put her mirror back into her bag. 'We've been through that,' she said, getting out of the car. 'You're not a young man any longer.' He raced the engine a little. 'Why don't you wear your gloves? Have you lost your gloves?' Walter Mitty reached in a pocket and brought out the gloves. He put them on, but after she had turned and gone into the building and he had driven on to a red light, he took them off again. 'Pick it up, brother!' snapped a cop as the light changed, and Mitty hastily pulled on his gloves and lurched ahead. He drove around the streets aimlessly for a time, and then he drove past the hospital on his way to the parking lot.

. . . 'It's the millionaire banker, Wellington McMillan,' said the pretty nurse. 'Yes?' said Walter Mitty, removing his gloves slowly. 'Who has the case?' 'Dr Renshaw and Dr Benbow, but there are two specialists here, Dr Remington from New York and Dr Pritchard-Mitford from London. He flew over.' A door opened down a long, cool corridor and Dr Renshaw came out. He looked distraught and haggard. 'Hello, Mitty,' he said. 'We're having the devil's own time with McMillan, the millionaire banker and close personal friend of Roosevelt. Obstrosis of the ductal tract. Tertiary. Wish you'd take a look at him.' 'Glad to,' said Mitty.

In the operating room there were whispered introductions: 'Dr Remington, Dr Mitty. Dr Pritchard-Mitford, Dr Mitty.' 'I've read your book on streptothricosis,' said Pritchard-Mitford, shaking hands. 'A briiliant performance, sir.' 'Thank you,' said Walter Mitty. 'Didn't know you were in the States, Mitty,' grumbled Remington. 'Coals to Newcastle, bringing Mitford and me up here for a tertiary.' 'You are very kind,' said Mitty. A huge, complicated machine, connected to the operating table, with many tubes and wires, began at this moment to go pocketa-pocketa-pocketa. 'The new anaesthetizer is giving away!' shouted an intern. 'There is no one in the East who knows how to fix it!' 'Quiet, man!' said Mitty, in a low, cool voice. He sprang to the machine, which was now going pocketa-pocketa-queep-pocketa-queep. He began fingering delicately a row of glistening dials. 'Give me a fountain pen!' he snapped. Someone handed him a fountain pen. He pulled a faulty piston out of the machine and inserted the pen in its place. 'That will hold for ten minutes,' he said. 'Get on with the operation.' A nurse hurried over and whispered to Renshaw, and Mitty saw the man turn pale. 'Coreopsis has set in,' said Renshaw nervously. 'If you would take over, Mitty?' Mitty looked at him and at the craven figure of Benbow, who drank, and at the grave, uncertain faces of the two great specialists. 'If you wish,' he said. They slipped a white gown on him; he adjusted a mask and drew on thin gloves; nurses handed him shining . . .

'Back it up, Mac! Look out for that Buick!' Walter Mitty jammed on the brakes. 'Wrong lane, Mac,' said the parking-lot attendant, looking at Mitty closely. 'Gee. Yeh,' muttered Mitty. He began cautiously to back out of the lane marked 'Exit Only.' 'Leave her sit there,' said the attendant. 'I'll put her away.' Mitty got out of the car. 'Hey, better leave the key.' 'Oh,' said Mitty, handing the man the ignition key. The attendant vaulted into the car, backed it up with insolent skill, and put it where it belonged.

They're so darn cocky, thought Walter Mitty, walking along Main Street; they think they know everything. Once he had tried to take his chains off, outside New Milford, and he had got them wound around the axles. A man had had to come out in a wrecking car and unwind them, a young, grinning garageman. Since then Mrs Mitty always made him drive to a garage to have the chains taken off. The next time, he thought, I'll wear my right arm in a sling; they won't grin at me then. I'll have my right arm in a sling and they'll see I couldn't possibly take the chains off myself. He kicked at the slush on the sidewalk. 'Overshoes,' he said to himself and he began looking for a shoe store.

When he came out into the street again, with the overshoes in a box under his

9

TEXT B

arm, Walter Mitty began to wonder what the other thing was his wife had told him to get. She had told him twice before they set out from their house for Waterbury. In a way he hated these weekly trips to town – he was always getting something wrong. Kleenex, he thought. Squibb's, razor blades? No. Toothpaste, toothbrush, bicarbonate, carborundum, initiative and referendum? He gave it up. But she would remember it. 'Where's the what's-its-name?' she would ask. 'Don't tell me you forgot the what's-its-name.' A newsboy went by shouting something about the Waterbury trial.

. . . 'Perhaps this will refresh your memory.' The District Attorney suddenly thrust a heavy automatic at the quiet figure on the witness stand. 'Have you ever seen this before?' Walter Mitty took the gun and examined it expertly. 'This is my Webley-Vickers 50.80,' he said calmly. An excited buzz ran around the courtroom. The Judge rapped for order. 'You are a crack shot with any sort of firearms, I believe?' said the District Attorney, insinuatingly. 'Objection!' shouted Mitty's attorney. 'We have shown that he wore his right arm in a sling on the night of the fourteenth of July.' Walter Mitty raised his hand briefly and the bickering attorneys were stilled. 'With any known make of gun,' he said evenly, 'I could have killed Gregory Fitzhurst at three hundred feet with my left hand.' Pandemonium broke loose in the courtroom. A woman's scream rose above the bedlam and suddenly a lovely, dark-haired girl was in Walter Mitty's arms. The District Attorney struck at her savagely. Without rising from his chair, Mitty let the man have it on the point of the chin. 'You miserable cur!' . . .

'Puppy biscuit,' said Walter Mitty. He stopped walking and the buildings of Waterbury rose up out of the misty courtroom and surrounded him again. A woman who was passing laughed. 'He said "Puppy biscuit,"' she said to her companion. 'That man said "Puppy biscuit" to himself.' Walter Mitty hurried on. He went into an A. & P., not the first one he came to but a smaller one farther up the street. 'I want some biscuit for small, young dogs,' he said to the clerk. 'Any special brand, sir?' The greatest pistol shot in the world thought a moment. 'It says "Puppies Bark for It" on the box,' said Walter Mitty.

His wife would be through at the hairdresser's in fifteen minutes, Mitty saw in looking at his watch, unless they had trouble drying it; sometimes they had trouble drying it. She didn't like to get to the hotel first; she would want him to be there waiting for her as usual. He found a big leather chair in the lobby, facing a window, and he put the overshoes and the puppy biscuit on the floor beside it. He picked up an old copy of *Liberty* and sank down into the chair. 'Can Germany Conquer the World Through the Air?' Walter Mitty looked at the pictures of bombing planes and of ruined streets.

. . . 'The cannonading has got the wind up in young Raleigh, sir,' said the sergeant. Captain Mitty looked up at him through tousled hair. 'Get him to bed,' he said wearily, 'with the others. I'll fly alone.' 'But you can't, sir,' said the sergeant anxiously. 'It takes two men to handle that bomber and the Archies are pounding hell out of the air. Von Richtman's circus is between here and Saulier.' 'Somebody's got to get that ammunition dump,' said Mitty. 'I'm going over. Spot of brandy?' He poured a drink for the sergeant and one for himself. War thundered and whined around the dugout and battered at the door. There was a rending of wood, and splinters flew through the room. 'A bit of a near thing,' said Captain Mitty carelessly. 'The box barrage is closing in,' said the sergeant. 'We only live once, Sergeant,' said Mitty, with his faint, fleeting smile. 'Or do we?' He poured another brandy and tossed it off. 'I never see a man could hold his brandy like you sir,' said the sergeant. 'Begging your pardon, sir.' Captain Mitty stood up and strapped on his huge Webley-Vickers automatic. 'It's forty kilometres through hell, sir,' said the sergeant. Mitty finished one last brandy. 'After all,' he said softly, 'what isn't?' The pounding of the cannon increased; there was the rat-tat-tatting of machine guns, and from somewhere came the menacing pocketa-pocketa-pocketa of the new flame throwers. Walter Mitty walked to the door of the dugout humming 'Auprès de Ma Blonde.' He turned and waved to the sergeant. 'Cheerio!' he said .

Something struck his shoulder. 'I've been looking all over this hotel for you,' said Mrs Mitty. 'Why do you have to hide in this old chair? How did you expect me to find you?' 'Things close in,' said Walter Mitty vaguely. 'What?' Mrs Mitty said. 'Did you get the what's-its-name? The puppy biscuit? What's that box?' 'Overshoes,' said Mitty. 'Couldn't you have put them on in the store?' 'I was thinking,' said Walter Mitty.'Does it ever occur to you that I am sometimes thinking?' She looked at him. 'I'm going to take your temperature when I get you home, she said.

They went out through the revolving doors that made a faintly derisive whistling sound when you pushed them. It was two blocks to the parking lot. At the drugstore on the corner she said, 'Wait here for me. I forgot something. I won't be a minute.' She was more than a minute. Walter Mitty lighted a cigarette. It began to rain, rain with sleet in it. He stood up against the wall of the drugstore smoking. . . . He put his shoulders back and his heels together. 'To hell with the handkerchief,' said Walter Mitty scornfully. He took one last drag on his cigarette and snapped it away. Then, with that faint, fleeting smile playing about his lips, he faced the firing squad; erect and motionless, proud and disdainful, Walter Mitty, the Undefeated, inscrutable to the last.

The Secret Life of Walter Mitty, James Thurber, Hamish Hamilton, 1942

10 NOT QUITE CLEAR

Text B

MISUNDERSTANDINGS From *Messing About With Problems* by C. Eden, S. Jones and D. Sims

If one had to choose a single problem that people in organisations bemoan more often than any others it would surely be the 'poor communication' and 'misunderstandings' that are pretty well endemic in all but the smallest and most stable organisations. But in referring to such occasions managers and administrators often imply that they result from no more than carelessness – and that in a well-run, professionally managed organisation such events would not occur. In fact, the issue runs far deeper than this as the following piece makes very plain. Consider the following account.

John Smith is a marketing manager in a division of a large manufacturing company; Ian Brown is the division's newly appointed marketing director. John Smith had just been to a meeting of the marketing department, the first with its new director. The appointment had not been a great surprise. Most people had assumed that Ian would get the job after his predecessor Brian Jones had been promoted to Head Office. In the three years since he had joined the division, Ian's area had been particularly successful, with two major and successful new product launches. He also had exactly the right kind of personality, John mused, aggressive, dynamic, self-confident. Personally, John did not like him and thought he could be an 'absolute bastard' at times, but John had to admit that he was good at this job. Furthermore, with the successor to Ian's old job still undecided it would be stupid to 'get on the wrong side' of the man, even if his own chances of getting the job were, at this stage, remote. Anyway, he thought, the meeting had not been the exciting event everyone had been expecting, although the fact that no announcements had been made about the successor would be bound to get everybody talking. In the meeting Ian had just gone over the future plans and there was nothing new, the usual policy statements about the fact that the division was strong in some markets, weak in others and efforts to find new products would continue to have a high priority.

Peter Williams, responsible for the industrial products section, had put forward his usual argument that the problems in his area had little to do with the division's (i.e. his) efforts and much more to do with overall adverse market conditions. There was no doubt that he was probably right and Ian had not openly disagreed, though he had cut Peter short in the middle of his 'spiel'. (Peter did tend to go on a bit.)

As John walked down the corridor Martin Evans, the promotions co-ordinator, came up to him. 'What did you think of that, then?' he asked. 'O.K.', John grunted, guardedly, turning into his office. Martin was one of those people he disliked and distrusted. His efforts to impress Ian in the meeting had been so obvious as to be almost amusing, John thought.

As John sat down Alan Dixon came in. Alan was the new-products manager and a good friend both in and outside work. He was looking anxious. 'Didn't like the sound of all that,' he said. 'I reckon we are all going to be under the microscope now. Did you notice how he looked at me when he said we should pay more attention to exploiting existing names in development?' (John hadn't.) 'You know how much trouble I had convincing Brian that we should keep separate identities for products in different marketing segments. I thought I had won that one. Now it looks as if I'll have to go through it all over again. I tell you, if he starts trying to change things radically in my area, it will be a disaster. And what about the way he was getting at Peter. I think he is definitely going to try to give Peter the push . . .'

We left John and his friend Alan in the middle of discussing what had 'gone on' in the meeting they had both just attended. It is clear that Alan had placed an interpretation upon the events occurring in that meeting, in terms of potential significance for him, quite different from that belonging to John. His interpretation had led him to feel distinctly anxious about the future behaviour of the new marketing director. John, on the other hand, had found the meeting rather uneventful. We may even suppose that he had been disappointed that it had not been more exciting. Are we 'rigging' the story? Of course. Yet we would ask you to consider how often when 'comparing notes' with colleagues after a meeting you find that each person will recall different aspects of the meeting, place different emphases on different aspects, or interpret the implications of the meeting in different ways. Sometimes the differences can be so significant that it hardly seems that the same meeting is being discussed.

The point that we wish to make here is so obvious that it appears almost trivial. Different people interpret situations in different ways. We have much in common with others in our social worlds – language, shared beliefs about the nature of things and relationships between them, and shared norms about what we should or should not do. Many of these come to have a meaning so institutionalised that they are taken to be 'matters of fact'. Nevertheless our individual histories are unique to each of us. Different people interpret situations in different ways because they bring to a situation their own particular mental 'framework' of personal beliefs, attitudes, hypotheses, prejudices, expectations, personal values and objectives, with which they can make sense of (place an interpretation upon) the situation. Thus they pay attention to certain things, ignore others, and regard some as having a particular significance for themselves in the future.

Returning to our example, this perspective would lead us to suggest that different recollections of a meeting by different individuals, have less to do with one person having a 'better' memory than another than with how those individuals differently made sense of the meeting in terms of their particular mental frameworks. That is to say, individuals' recollections of a meeting and interpretations of what was significant within it come from their own beliefs and expectations – for example, about the world of things and people in general, about meetings in their organisation, about the people there and their intentions – and from the future implications they see in the meeting for themselves in terms of their values and objectives.

Messing About with Problems, C. Eden, S. Jones and D. Sims, Pergamon Press, 1983

INDEX

ALPHABETICAL INDEX OF TOPICS, FUNCTIONS AND GRAMMAR POINTS

A

academic subjects, discussion of specialties etc. 9.B1
aim VP 3.D1
almost 7B.6(b)
ambiguity 10.B6, 7
aphorisms 1.B5, 8.B3
APPOSITION 1.B6, D1
approving, expressing approval 6.D
are to (do) 6.D2
articles 5.D5
as if 9.B3
assume VP 10.D3
attention, focusing attention 5.D1
avoiding responsibility for actions (e.g. by using a passive structure) 4.D3

B

better (had better) 7.D3
body language 3.B4,6
bother VP 4.D1

C

can do with VP 4.D1
causes, *adducing causes* 3.B2, 4.B2(a), 7.B1
challenging, challenging assumptions 3.2(d)
clarification, asking for clarification 10.B1, 10.D4
CLEFT SENTENCES 8.B2, 8.B3, 8.D2
comparing 2.B2, B4, 6.B1, 6.B3
comparing (past + present) 2.B3, 2.B5, 3.B5, 4.B1
COMPOUNDS (open) 1.D3
compromising, making compromises 1.B4
conclude VP 9.D1
CONDITIONALS 1,3   3.D3, 3.E
confusions and misunderstandings 10.D2, 10.D3
connotations 9.B4
contrasting 2
could have (done) (criticism) 6.D2
criticising 6.D

D

daydreams 9.B3(b)
deduce VP 9.D1
deducing 3.B4
despite 2.D1
disapproving 6.D
disarmers 2.DB(b), 7.B5
dislikes 4.22
distinctions, *drawing distinctions* 2.B2(c), (d)
doubt 10.B2
dreams 9.B3(a)
duties 5.B2

E

ELLIPSIS 4.B4, D2
EMPHASISERS 8.D2
emphasising 8
enquiring 6.B3 1
enthusiasm, *responding enthusiastically to offers etc.* 8.D3
enumerating 1.A, 1.B2
even if 2.D1
even though 2.D1
EXCLAMATORY sentences (What a ...!) 8.D2
expect VP 10.D3

F

fail VP 4.D1
fields of study, academic subjects, specialties. 9.B1
first impressions 8.B1
focusing attention (particularly, solely, specially etc.) 5.D4
FOREIGN PLURALS 5.E
forget VP 4.D1, 10.D3
friendship 7.A
FUTURE CONTINUOUS 10.B1
FUTURE IN THE PAST 7.D1

G

generalising 5.B4
GERUND (passive) 4.B2(b)
'GET' PASSIVE 4.D3

good at + ing 4.B2
groups and organisations 4.B1(c)

H
hardly 7.B6(b)
human failings 4.B2(a)
human qualities (and their negative sides) 7.B3

I
ideologies 6.B1
if only 4.B2(c), D1
imagine VP 9.B3(a),(b)
imply VP 9.D1
impressions of people 8.B1
indignation, *expressing indignation* 6.D1, 6.D2
in case 3.D4
-ING FORM (passive gerund) 4.B2(b)
-ING FORM (present participle) 3.D4
in spite of 2.D1
intelligence (varieties of) 2.B2(c),(d),(e)
intend VP 3.D1
INTENSIFIERS 8.D2
interviews 8.B1(b),(c)
INVERSION (Only . . . Under no circumstances . . . etc.) 8.D2, 8.E
invitations (adjusting according to recipients) (See 9.D3 for pre-invitations) 6.B3(c),(d)
involve VP 3.D1
IRREGULAR PLURALS 5.E
irritation, *expressing irritation* 6.D2
IT (CLEFT SENTENCES) (e.g. 'It's money that matters') 8.B3
it's better to . . . 3.B1

J
jargon 10.B3

L
love 1.A, 1.B1, 1.B5

M
make (somebody do) 3.B1
may 10.D1
mean VP 3.D1
might 3.B2, 10.D1
might well 10.D1
misunderstandings 10.D3
MODALS 3.B1, 3.B2(d), 3.B4, 5.B1, 2, 10.D1

MODALS (past) 7.B1
must 3.B4(a), 3.B4(c)

N
necessitate VP 3.B2(c)
negative responses to requests 7.B4
NEGATIVES (anomalous or difficult examples) 7.D3
nevertheless 2.D1
no, *ways of saying no* 7.B4
NON-DEFINING RELATIVES 1.D1

O
OPEN COMPOUNDS (e.g. fuel consumption) 1.D3
ought 3.B1, 5.B1, 5.B2

P
PARTICIPLES (present and past) 3.D(d)
PARTICULARISERS (e.g. chiefly, mainly, especially) 5.D4
PASSIVE (+ get) 4.D3
PASSIVE GERUND 4.B2(b)
PASSIVES 4.B2(b), 4.D3
past and present compared 4.B1, 3.B5
PAST PERFECT (+ if only, wish) 4.B3, 4.D1
perplexity, *expressing perplexity* 6.D2
PLURALS (irregular and compound) 5.E
politics 6.B1
PRE-INVITATIONS 6.B3(c),(d)
PREFIXES 1.E
prejudice 6.B2
prevent VP 3.D4
priorities 8.B4
PSEUDO-CLEFT sentences (What we want is . . .) 8.B2, 8.D2

Q
qualities of mind 9.B2

R
rather (I'd rather you . . . + verb) 7.B4, 7.D1
realise VP 10.D3
regret VP 4.D1
relationships 1.A, 1.B1, 1.B2
RELATIVES (non-defining) 1.D1
requesting 9.D2, 6.B3(d)
responding (to offers, invitations, suggestions and enquiries) 8.D3
responsibility (*avoiding responsibility* for

an action by e.g. using a passive structure) 4.D3
rights and duties 5.B2

S
scenarios 3.B2(c)
should 3.B1, 10.B2
should (criticism) 6.D2
supposed to 6.D2

T
tentativeness, *expressing tentativeness* 3.B2(b)

U
unless 3.D4
unlike 2.D1

unwillingness, *expressing degrees of unwillingness* 7.B4
used to (do) 3.B5

V
visual representation of information (e.g. graphs) 3.B3

W
WHAT in exclamatory sentences (e.g. What a smart suit you're wearing!) 8.D2
WHAT in pseudo-cleft sentences (What we need is time) 8.B2, 8.D2
whereas 2.D(a)
wish (+ past perfect) 4.B3, 4.D1, 6.D2
wordplay 10.B4, B5